INVESTING 101

A BEGINNER-FRIENDLY GUIDE TO INVESTING IN THE STOCK MARKET, INDEX FUNDS, REITS, RENTAL PROPERTIES, CRYPTO, AND MORE—BUILD A POWERFUL, DIVERSIFIED PORTFOLIO WITH MINIMAL RISK AND EFFORT

LUCAS STERLING

TOP TIER PRESS

Published under the author brand **Lucas Sterling**

CONTENTS

INTRODUCTION

Do you remember the first time someone told you about investing? Maybe you pictured crowded stock exchanges with people in suits or imagined you needed thousands of dollars just to get started. For a lot of us, investing can seem like something reserved for the ultra-wealthy, people with finance degrees, or those who read The Wall Street Journal over their morning coffee. But here's an important truth: investing isn't just for 'them.' It's for you — whether you're a college student learning how to stretch your paycheck, a freelancer eager to grow your side hustle savings, or someone who's simply curious about building a brighter financial future.

To start investing, you don't need a specific job title, a significant amount of spare cash, or years of research experience. You need the courage to learn and take the first step, even if it feels scary. No matter where you're starting from, this book is designed to guide you, at your speed, toward real financial empowerment. If you've ever felt overwhelmed by confusing jargon or found yourself believing that investing is risky, complicated, and out of reach, you're not alone. These are common myths that hold far too many people back from taking control of their money.

Let's address one of the biggest obstacles right away: the fear that you don't know enough to invest wisely. Maybe you've heard stories about friends who lost money in the stock market, or perhaps news headlines make investing sound unpredictable and scary. Here's what you might not realize: not investing comes with its own set of risks, ones that are far more certain over the long term.

Take a moment to think about what happens when you leave your money sitting in a regular savings account. It feels safe, right? The money is there whenever you need it, and you might even earn a little bit of interest. But while your balance sits quietly, something else is happening behind the scenes — something called inflation. Every year, prices for things like groceries, rent, and transportation tend to go up, sometimes by only a small amount, sometimes by much more. Over time, this means the money you worked hard to save actually buys less and less. That $1,000 you put away today might be worth just $900, or even less, in real purchasing power ten years from now.

What does this mean for your dreams — owning a home, traveling, retiring comfortably, or simply enjoying freedom from financial stress? It means that relying solely on traditional savings accounts or stashing cash under your mattress isn't enough to keep pace with your life goals. Growing your wealth isn't just about accumulating money; it's about protecting your future self from missed opportunities. And that's where investing comes in.

Investing is often misunderstood as a gamble or a luxury. In reality, it is one of the smartest, most practical tools available to anyone who wants to shape a secure and meaningful future. When you invest, you put your money to work so you don't have to work forever. Thanks to the power of compounding — the process by which your investments generate returns, and then those returns generate even more returns over time — even small, consistent steps add up to significant progress. You don't need to start with large sums of money or proprietary knowledge. Whether you can set aside $5 a week or a few hundred dollars a month, you have options. Investing involves taking a long-term perspective, making well-informed decisions, and allowing time to take its course.

So why haven't more people embraced investing early? One reason is that myths and misinformation are everywhere. Maybe you've been told that investing is only for people with extra income to spare. Maybe you believe that if you're not a math whiz or a financial planner, you're bound to make costly mistakes. Or maybe you simply feel like all the talk about stocks, bonds, and mutual funds sounds like a foreign language. These beliefs are understandable, but they're also outdated. The truth is, most successful investors started out just as uncertain as you might feel right now.

Throughout this book, we'll break down these barriers together. You will learn why investing is not just possible but essential, regardless of your current financial situation or background. We'll translate unfamiliar terms into plain English and focus on practical steps that fit your lifestyle. Whether you have a steady job, juggle multiple gigs, are paying off student loans, or are saving for a big goal, there's a place for you in the world of investing. You do not need to have a lot of money to begin. You do not need to understand every corner of the market before taking action. What you do need is a willingness to move beyond old fears — and a commitment to your future.

Imagine feeling confident when opening your banking app, seeing your investments steadily growing, and knowing you're actively creating choices for yourself down the road. Think about being able to support causes you care about, take career risks, or retire earlier than you thought possible. None of this requires perfection. All it takes is a mindset shift and a little guidance, which you'll find in the pages ahead.

Here's what you can expect as you move through this book: First, you'll discover why investing matters — not just for Wall Street, but for everyday people trying to get ahead. We'll explore the real impact of inflation, show you why keeping money in low-interest accounts may be costing you more than you realize, and share stories of individuals who started with modest sums and saw life-changing results. Along the way, you'll find powerful evidence to replace old myths with new facts. By the end of our journey, you'll be equipped to recognize opportunities, weigh risks smartly, and make choices that align with your unique goals.

This book is your toolkit for changing the way you think about money and your ability to build wealth. Each chapter is crafted to meet you where you are, offering straightforward advice without overwhelming you. You'll find checklists, examples, and practical tips to help you take concrete steps — at your pace — toward a more secure future. You have the power to decide how quickly and how far you want to venture into the world of investing.

Ultimately, my goal is to help you feel prepared — not just to invest, but to take charge of your entire financial journey. No more feeling stuck or intimidated by complicated systems. Together, we'll simplify the process, clear away confusion, and put the power back in your hands. Investing is for everyone, and that includes you.

Welcome to a new chapter in your financial story. Let's begin.

UNLOCK YOUR FINANCIAL FREEDOM BLUEPRINT

Ready to turn your financial goals into real, actionable progress?

As a thank-you for reading this book, I've created a powerful companion resource: **The Financial Freedom Blueprint**. This exclusive, step-by-step guide helps you identify your ideal money path, plug income leaks, and make smart, aligned decisions fast. It's designed to take you from financial confusion to confidence in just a few focused steps.

What's included in this resource:

- Clarify your goals
- Streamline your expenses
- Align your spending with your values
- Start building real wealth now!

👉 **Access Your Financial Blueprint Today**
Visit: **https://content.toptierpress.com/unlock-financial-freedom**

Or scan the QR code below to get instant access!

ONE
THE BUILDING BLOCKS OF INVESTING

Have you ever wondered what it really means to invest, or why some people seem to grow their money steadily over time while others struggle to get ahead? Maybe you've heard the term "compound interest" tossed around but aren't quite sure how it works or why it matters. Or perhaps you feel uncertain about how much risk is too much when putting your money into stocks, bonds, or other opportunities. If these questions sound familiar, you're not alone.

Many adults starting out with investing face the same challenges — figuring out where to begin, understanding the balance between risk and reward, and learning how to make their money work for them without constant supervision. This chapter will help you build a solid foundation by explaining key concepts: what investing truly is, how compounding accelerates growth, why aligning risk with your comfort level matters, and what types of income different investments can generate. With clear examples and straightforward language, you'll gain the confidence to approach investing thoughtfully and take greater control of your financial future.

UNDERSTANDING INVESTING AND THE POWER OF COMPOUND INTEREST

Investing is putting your money to work so it can grow. Instead of allowing your cash to remain idle in your bank account while earning minimal interest, consider using it in ways that could generate higher returns. At its heart, investing is about making your money help you build wealth rather than only relying on your paycheck.

Picture someone who likes a particular company, maybe one that makes eco-friendly products. They believe this company will sell more in the future and make greater profits. By buying shares, or pieces of the company, this person becomes a partial owner. If the company does well, its value can increase, and so does the value of the shares. If the company also pays a portion of its profits to shareholders through dividends, that's an extra reward on top of any price increase.

Consider someone else who buys a house with the idea of renting it out. The rent each month provides regular income, while over the years the house could rise in value. If the owner sells it for more than they bought it for, that's an additional profit.

Think about bonds, which are like loans you give to governments or companies. In exchange for lending your money, they agree to pay you interest regularly and return your original investment later. Many people like bonds because of their steady stream of income.

There are also those who might invest by starting a small business — a coffee shop on a busy street, for example. The money spent on the shop is an investment. If the coffee shop thrives, profits can be much larger than the original amount put in.

What sets investing apart from saving is the way your money behaves. Saving is like storing your cash in a box — it stays safe but doesn't do much. When you invest, your money is actively working for you in the world. For example, if you put aside $1,000 in a savings account that pays 0.5% interest per year, you'll have $1,005 at the end of the year. But if you invest that same $1,000 in a business or shares in a growing company, you have a chance of making much more, even though there's some risk involved.

Take the case of a rideshare driver who wants to build a safety net. If they put away a portion of each week's earnings in a high-interest account or buy a small number of shares every month, their money isn't just set aside — it's potentially positioned to grow. Gig workers, freelancers, and young professionals often need their money to stretch further, and investing helps by offering the potential for higher returns than simple saving.

The driving force behind wealth growth in investing is the extra income it can generate. When you buy a rental property, those monthly payments from tenants start adding up, and over time, so does the property's value. When you hold shares in a company, you might receive dividends and watch your investment grow in value. What really accelerates wealth is reinvesting those returns — using the extra income from investments to make even more investments. It's like planting seeds that keep giving fruit and using some of that fruit to plant even more seeds.

There's a big difference between investing for quick wins versus thinking long term. Some individuals aim to achieve success by strategically timing the market or following rapidly evolving trends. But real wealth tends to grow over years, not days. This long-term perspective enables compound interest to function effectively.

Compound interest is when your earnings themselves start earning money. Imagine you invest $1,000 in a fund that grows at 7% each year. After one year, you'd have $1,070. Instead of taking out the extra $70, you leave it invested, so the next year it's 7% of $1,070, giving you $1,144.90. Year after year, your investment grows faster because you're earning returns not just on the money you put in, but also on all the profits that have built up. See how those numbers stack up over time:

Year	Value at 7% Growth
1	$1,070
5	$1,403
10	$1,967
20	$3,870

Starting early is important because compound growth gets stronger with time. Small amounts can grow into substantial sums if left invested and allowed to build on themselves.

There are many reasons people invest. Some want security for the future, like saving for retirement. Others hope to buy a home or pay for a child's education. Common places to put investment money include shares of companies, bonds, real estate, and starting or investing in businesses. Each works in a slightly different way, but all share the goal of turning today's money into more tomorrow.

Investing is simple: choose where to put your money, watch how it performs, and decide when to use your gains. Time is one of your most powerful tools. The longer you let investments grow, the more chance they have of multiplying. But every opportunity comes with its set of risks, and weighing them is always part of the investing journey.

BALANCING RISK AND REWARD: FINDING YOUR COMFORT ZONE

Investing often feels like putting your money on a see-saw. On one side, you find safety and certainty, but likely with small returns. On the other, you have chances for higher returns, but with the risk that things might not go as planned. This balance is called risk versus reward, and every investor must decide where they feel comfortable sitting.

In the world of investing, risk means the likelihood that you could lose money or that your investment won't do as well as you hoped. For example, placing your money in a savings account is very safe. The big banks rarely fail, so you can be sure your money will be there tomorrow. But the trade-off is that your money grows very slowly — barely more than a few pennies for each dollar over a year. This is low risk, low reward.

Consider another option: stocks. When you buy a stock, you become a part-owner in a company. If the company does well, so does your investment. It can grow quickly, sometimes doubling or tripling in a few years. But the company could also face problems and its value may drop, which means you could lose part of your investment. This is higher risk, higher potential reward.

Risk comes in many forms. It's not just about losing money because a company goes out of business. Some of the most common risks include:

Risk Categories in Investments

Risk Type	What It Means	Example
Market Risk	The chance your investment goes down because the market drops	Stock prices fall during an economic slump
Inflation Risk	The danger that rising prices will eat into your investment's value	Low-yield bonds may not keep up with inflation
Liquidity Risk	The risk that you can't quickly convert your investment into cash	Selling real estate can take months

Each type of investment carries its own mix of these risks. For example, government bonds are less affected by market ups and downs, and you can usually sell them quickly, so they carry less risk overall. But they don't pay much and may not keep up with inflation. Cryptocurrencies, on the other hand, change value quickly, are harder to predict, and might be tough to sell in a panic. The potential for big gains is there, but so is the chance of big losses.

Deciding how much risk to take should start with a look at your own financial situation and feelings about loss. This is called risk tolerance

— how much you're willing to stomach the ups and downs. Some people happily ride out wild swings in the hope of bigger gains. Others want to sleep well at night knowing their money is safe, even if it grows slowly.

Assessing Your Risk Tolerance

A few questions can help you decide where you stand:

- How would you feel if your investment lost 20% of its value in a year?
- Are you counting on this money soon, or can you leave it untouched for five years or more?
- Do you have stable income and savings to fall back on?
- What are your problems and goals — growing wealth, saving for a house, or planning for retirement?

Risk tolerance depends on personal factors. Younger investors sometimes accept more risk because they have time to recover from losses. Someone older, or planning to buy a home soon, may need to be more careful. Stable jobs and steady income let you handle more ups and downs. If you depend on your investments for daily living, playing it safe is generally better.

Matching Investments to Your Comfort Zone

Picture two friends, Amy and Ben. Amy is 25, starting her first job, and wants long-term growth to buy a home in ten years. She can handle more risk, so her portfolio holds mostly stocks and some bonds. Ben, 50, earns a good salary but wants to retire soon. He's more cautious, putting his savings mainly in government bonds and some savings accounts.

Diversifying across different types of investments can also spread risk. Instead of betting everything on one company or property, spreading money into stocks, bonds, savings, and maybe a small slice of something riskier like real estate or mutual funds helps cushion losses if one part falls behind. This mix helps manage risk while still offering room for growth over time.

Passive income strategies reward patience with steady returns. Investments in dividend-paying stocks or rental properties may offer fewer wild swings but provide ongoing cash flow. High-yield savings accounts create slow, reliable growth. Each method fits a unique risk/reward preference, emphasizing that there's no single right answer. The important part is knowing your comfort zone, assessing your priorities, and choosing matching investments you can stick with.

PASSIVE VS. ACTIVE INCOME: BUILDING WEALTH THROUGH INVESTING

Many people dream of waking up to money earned while they slept. This is the promise behind passive income, which stands in contrast to active income — each playing a different role in the journey toward financial independence. Understanding how they differ, and how investing helps transition from one to the other, is crucial for crafting a sustainable wealth-building plan.

Active income refers to money you receive in exchange for your effort, time, or skills. Consider a freelance web designer who gets paid per project or a young professional working a full-time job for a monthly salary. If they stop working, their income halts. This exchange of hours for dollars means your earning potential is bound tightly to the hours you can physically or mentally contribute. Side hustles, like pet-sitting or driving for a rideshare service, also fall under active income. They may fit flexibly into your schedule, but they still require presence and energy.

Passive income operates differently. It's income generated with minimal day-to-day involvement. For example, when a web designer invests in a small apartment and rents it out, the monthly rent payments become passive income. Another scenario involves purchasing shares in a company — receiving dividend payments without doing the daily work of running the business. These income streams typically require upfront work, capital, or creativity but continue generating money with little ongoing attention.

Passive income streams are pivotal for long-term financial growth because they help to decouple your earning capacity from your time. As life circumstances change, having income that isn't directly tied to hours worked increases flexibility. In retirement, or during a career break, passive earnings can maintain your standard of living. For side-hustlers or freelancers facing inconsistent workloads, passive income provides a financial cushion and peace of mind when active projects slow down.

Establishing passive income sources usually requires a significant initial effort. Purchasing a rental property demands research, legal paperwork, and sometimes renovation. Creating a digital course or self-published eBook involves a heavy burst of upfront creativity and technical work before it can generate ongoing sales. Even investing in dividend stocks or real estate investment trusts (REITs) means researching, choosing, and managing investments and reviewing performance periodically. Passive income is rarely effortless at the outset — success often comes down to the quality of the initial setup and the diligence invested in risk assessment.

A few traditional passive income opportunities available through investing include:

- Rental real estate: Buying property and earning income through monthly rent payments
- Dividend-paying stocks: Earning a share of company profits regularly, just for holding stock
- Peer-to-peer lending: Funding loans for other individuals or businesses in exchange for regular interest payments
- REITs: Investing in real estate portfolios that pay out a portion of proceeds as dividends

These avenues illustrate that investing acts as an entry point for making your money work for you. The degree of direct involvement still varies. Owning a single-family home and acting as a landlord can be more management-intensive than investing in a mutual fund, where your role is mostly to monitor and rebalance your portfolio.

The relationship between effort, time investment, and income potential is central to both income types. Active income may deliver faster returns when starting out — a freelance writing gig pays within weeks, while investment property might not yield positive cash flow for months. Passive income, on the other hand, can compound over time; a diversified portfolio steadily grows through reinvested dividends or appreciation in property value. However, the time it takes to build meaningful passive income streams is often underestimated, as is the persistence and learning curve involved.

Evaluating passive income opportunities involves looking closely at risk, potential returns, and personal resources — skills, capital, and available time. A side-hustler with marketing expertise might build a blog that earns ad revenue, while someone with savings might prefer dividend stocks or REITs. Key questions to ask include: What is the minimum investment? How stable is this source of income? What risks could disrupt it? How easily can it scale if I want to increase my returns?

Diversification becomes crucial, both as a safeguard and as a way to expand total passive income. Instead of relying on a single rental property, investing in different asset classes — like stocks, real estate, and digital products — mitigates the risk of one stream failing. For young professionals, balancing a few manageable passive sources alongside active work is a realistic path to stability.

Passive income is sometimes thought of as a myth or "easy money," yet most people discover it's built on consistent effort, wise investing, and a patient mindset. Recognizing the benefits and limitations of both active and passive income allows everyone — from freelancers to full-time employees — to better match their resources to income opportunities and to lay the groundwork for financial security and freedom.

Now that we have explored the core ideas of investing — from how your money can grow through compound interest to finding a balance between risk and reward and understanding the difference between active and passive income — you are better prepared to take the next step. With this foundation, you can begin making informed choices about where to put your money, tailored to your goals, comfort with risk, and lifestyle. Remember, investing is not about quick wins but steady growth over time, giving you the power to build financial security and create income streams that work for you. As you move forward, keep learning, stay patient, and use these principles to shape a plan that fits your unique journey toward financial independence.

TWO
LAYING YOUR FINANCIAL GROUNDWORK

Have you ever found yourself wondering where your money goes each month, despite earning a steady paycheck or juggling multiple gigs? Perhaps you feel like saving or investing is out of reach because bills and expenses appear to pile up faster than you can keep track. For many adults starting their financial journeys, the challenge isn't just making money — it's understanding how to manage it well enough to build something lasting.

Setting clear goals and knowing how much to save or invest feels overwhelming when the basics aren't in place. Without a solid handle on your budget, unexpected costs, or growing debt, investing can seem risky or confusing. This chapter will guide you through establishing a strong financial foundation by mastering budgeting, protecting yourself from emergencies, handling debts intelligently, and aligning your investment plans with your personal goals and timelines. Taking these steps first helps turn scattered income into intentional growth, creating confidence and control as you begin building your financial future.

MASTERING BUDGETING TO FIND INVESTMENT CAPITAL

Earning money is only the first step; knowing exactly how much reaches your bank account each month lays the foundation for smart budgeting. If you work a regular nine-to-five, your paycheck may be steady, but it's still worth adding up your total income — after taxes — before making any plans. Freelancers and gig workers should average their earnings from the past several months to establish a reliable baseline. Even if income varies, reviewing your lowest-earning month helps you create a "worst-case scenario" budget that protects you from overspending.

Once your monthly income is clear, the next step is tracking expenses. Start by gathering statements from your bank, credit cards, or budgeting apps. List every regular bill — rent, utilities, phone, subscriptions, insurance, groceries, and transportation. Then add variable expenses: dining out, entertainment, shopping, and other costs that fluctuate. Whether you prefer pen and paper, a spreadsheet, or a digital app like Mint or You Need a Budget (YNAB), consistency is what matters most. Many people find that a simple spreadsheet with columns for "Income," "Fixed Expenses," and "Variable Expenses" keeps everything organized and easy to review.

After tracking a full month of spending, patterns begin to emerge. Maybe your coffee runs total $45 a month, or you're still paying for a streaming service you rarely use. This is where budgeting shifts from passive record-keeping to an active tool. Beside each category, mark expenses as "Needs," "Wants," or "Could Cut." These distinctions make it clear which costs are essential and which ones offer opportunities to redirect money toward your goals. For example:

Category	Amount	Type	Change
Rent	$800	Need	–
Groceries	$200	Need	–
Streaming	$15	Want	Could Cut
Restaurants	$90	Want	Reduce
Gym	$25	Need	–
Ride Shares	$30	Want	Reduce

This clear format helps visualize where money can be redirected. Maybe by skipping two restaurant dinners and dropping a streaming site, you free up $40 each month.

To make budgeting work long-term, consider using the 50/30/20 rule. Under this system, 50% of your after-tax income covers "Needs," 30% goes to "Wants," and the remaining 20% is dedicated to "Savings/Investing." For someone earning $2,000 monthly, the breakdown would look like this:

- Needs: $1,000
- Wants: $600
- Savings/Investing: $400

Plugging these percentages into your spreadsheet or app keeps spending in check and ensures investing happens every month. Digital tools with "goal" features, like PocketGuard or YNAB, even let you assign your investing amount as a recurring monthly target, giving you a clear number to hit.

Life isn't always predictable, and budgets need flexibility. If some months bring extra freelance work or overtime, decide in advance how much of that windfall will bolster investments. On the other hand, if your work is seasonal and some months are lean, setting aside buffer funds in better months can even things out. For irregular expenses like car maintenance or holiday gifts, estimate the annual cost, divide by twelve, and save that amount each month, smoothing out the bumps.

As your budget takes shape, the power of small changes emerges. Let's say you find $30 a month to invest — maybe that's a couple fewer movie tickets or resisting one impulse buy. Over a year, that adds up to $360. If invested regularly, those small sums grow — not just from your contributions, but from investment growth over time. It's easy to overlook these "extra" dollars when they're sitting in checking accounts, but tracking turns them into opportunities.

Imagine Sarah, a young professional with a $2,600 monthly take-home pay. Before budgeting, her savings account rarely grew. After tracking her spending, she realized $120 a month vanished on rideshares and food delivery. Cutting back to public transit and cooking three extra dinners weekly freed up $85 a month. She set up an automatic transfer — $50 to a basic investment account and $35 toward emergency savings. By the end of the year, she'd invested $600 and saved $420, all without feeling deprived.

Budgeting uncovers not just investment potential but also any gaps in emergency funds or warning signs of growing debt. Seeing a negative balance or frequent overdrafts is a prompt to cut more deeply or seek extra income before committing to investments. Proper budgets build confidence — making saving, spending, and investing intentional, not accidental. Each dollar you redirect strengthens your financial safety net and lays the groundwork for future growth.

BUILDING YOUR FINANCIAL SHIELD: EMERGENCY FUNDS AND DEBT MANAGEMENT

Unexpected expenses often arise when least expected, making it vital to build protection before investing. A solid financial shield is created through two key elements: maintaining an emergency fund and managing debt wisely. These act as buffers, protecting you from life's uncertainties while laying the groundwork for future investment success.

Understanding Emergency Funds

An emergency fund is money set aside specifically for genuine financial emergencies — situations you cannot predict or avoid. True emergencies include job loss, unexpected medical bills, urgent home or car repairs, or family crises that require immediate attention and resources. Non-emergencies are expenses you can plan for, like vacations, new gadgets, or sale events. Recognizing this difference helps avoid depleting your savings for nonessential reasons.

To determine the right size for your emergency fund, calculate your essential monthly expenses: rent or mortgage, utilities, groceries, transportation, insurance, and minimum debt payments. Multiply this total by three to six months as your target range. For example, if your monthly expenses total $2,500, then an emergency fund should fall between $7,500 and $15,000. A single person with stable employment may lean towards three months, while someone with dependents or variable income may choose the higher end.

Building your emergency fund rarely happens overnight. Instead, treat it as a goal to achieve in small, regular steps. Start by budgeting a set portion of your income each month, even if it's just $50 or $100. Set up an automatic transfer to a dedicated savings account, so the money moves before you spend it elsewhere. Celebrate milestones to stay motivated, such as reaching your first $500 or $1,000.

Accessibility is the main priority for emergency savings, not high returns. The money needs to be readily available when needed, so keep your fund in a high-yield savings account or a money market account. Avoid investing your emergency fund in stocks or other assets where its value could fluctuate or where withdrawals might take days to process.

Debt Management: Types and Strategies

Debt comes in many forms, but not all debt is created equal. High-interest debt — such as credit card balances, payday loans, and some personal loans — can quickly grow out of control if left unchecked.

Manageable debt includes low-interest student loans, mortgages, and some car loans, especially when payments fit comfortably in your budget and interest rates are moderate.

Prioritizing which debts to pay down first is crucial. Focus on high-interest debts before low-interest ones. Credit cards, often charging between 16% and 25% interest, cost you much more over time than the 3% to 5% you might pay on a mortgage. If you owe $5,000 on a credit card at 20% interest, you'll pay $1,000 a year just in interest. Compare this to potential investment returns: if your investments are projected to earn 7%, but your debt costs you 20%, you're actually losing money by investing rather than paying off this debt.

Some believe you can start investing immediately, even with high-interest debt, but this often erodes the benefits of your investments. It's typically wiser to eliminate these expensive debts first, then move to investing once you're spending less on interest and have reduced financial stress.

Several proven strategies help reduce debt effectively:

- **Avalanche Method:** Pay minimums on all debts, then put any extra money toward the debt with the highest interest rate.
- **Snowball Method:** Pay minimums on all debts, then target the smallest balance first to gain momentum from early wins.
- **Debt Consolidation:** Combine your debts into one loan with a lower overall interest rate for easier management.

A table helps illustrate these strategies:

Method	Focuses On	Pros	Cons
Avalanche	Highest interest	Saves most on interest	May take longer to see progress
Snowball	Smallest balance	Quick wins boost motivation	May pay more in interest
Consolidation	All debts into one	Streamlines payments, possible savings	Qualification required

How Emergency Funds and Debt Work Together

Imagine you start investing without an emergency fund. Suddenly, an unexpected car repair arises, costing $1,200. With no cash reserve, you swipe your credit card, adding to a balance with 22% interest. This new debt means future investment contributions have to cover both interest losses and possible lost investment growth.

With an emergency fund, the repair is paid promptly, and investments remain untouched and growing. Emergency funds also reduce stress and keep you from selling investments at a loss during a crisis.

A balanced approach often works best while building your foundation. For instance, if you have $300 a month to spare, you might put $200 toward credit card debt and $100 toward growing your emergency savings. This steady effort builds protection and steadily reduces liability, ensuring you're ready to invest confidently when the time comes.

Common myths suggest any savings are enough or that investing should always come first. In truth, a proper emergency fund and smart debt management provide the foundation for safe, sustainable investing. They enable you to navigate financial challenges, prevent additional debt, and enter the world of investing with assurance and stability.

DEFINING FINANCIAL GOALS AND ALIGNING THEM WITH TIME HORIZONS

When setting financial goals, the timeline for when you'll need the money is just as important as the amount. In investing, this timeline is called your "time horizon." Different time horizons shape your investment choices and the amount of risk you should consider. Time horizons generally fall into three categories: short-term, medium-term, and long-term.

Short-term goals mean you expect to use the money within three years. Common examples include saving for a vacation, building an emergency fund, or putting money aside for a car. Protecting this money from unexpected losses is crucial because we will need it soon. Even small downturns in the market can hurt if you need your funds quickly. That's why those with short-term goals usually focus on low-risk investments like savings accounts, certificates of deposit (CDs), or high-yield money market funds. These vehicles tend to offer modest returns but very little risk.

Medium-term goals are those with a three- to ten-year time frame. Examples are saving for a house down payment in five years, planning for a wedding, or building a college fund for a child who is starting elementary school. This period is long enough to consider more growth-focused investments but not so long that you can fully ignore risk. Investors often balance stable options with higher-return possibilities, such as a mix of bonds and conservative stock funds. This approach allows some room for ups and downs, with time to bounce back from moderate setbacks but not from severe losses.

Long-term goals look ten years or more into the future. Retirement is the classic example, but so are funding a newborn's college education or creating lasting wealth for your family. Over these extended timelines, you can weather the short-term fluctuations of the stock market. History shows that while stocks might occasionally drop sharply, they have trended upward over longer spans. For instance, according to the S&P 500's performance between 1926 and 2023, the average annual return was about 10%. While that doesn't mean every year was positive, it illustrates the long-term growth potential. Because of this, long-term investors are generally able to take on more risk by investing a larger portion of their money in stocks and stock-based funds.

There is no universal risk tolerance. Some individuals experience sleeplessness due to minor losses, whereas others don't mind fluctuations if they anticipate a larger future reward. However, your investment time horizon can help guide what amount of risk is appropriate. If you need your money soon, it's usually best to avoid riskier investments. If your goal is years away, you may have more capacity to handle short-term losses in exchange for greater possible gains.

Linking your goals to the right time horizon gives your plan structure. It can help to use a simple table or list like this:

Goal	When Needed	Time Horizon	Ideal Options
Buy a car	1 year	Short-term	Savings account, CD, money market
Down payment on house	5 years	Medium-term	Bond funds, balanced portfolios
College for newborn	18 years	Long-term	Stock funds, index funds
Open a business	2 years	Short-term	Cash, short-duration bonds
Retirement	30 years	Long-term	Stock funds, retirement accounts

To get started, make a list of your specific goals and estimate when you'll need the money for each. Assign each goal to one of the time horizon categories. Consider your own feelings about risk and use that understanding to choose investments that feel comfortable.

Another key concept is compound interest. Money you invest earns returns, and over time, those returns can generate even more returns, creating a snowball effect. For instance, if you invest $10,000 in a stock fund with an average annual return of 8%, after 3 years (short-term) you'll have about $12,600. Over 10 years (medium-term), the amount grows to nearly $21,600, and in 30 years (long-term), it can balloon to over $100,000. This shows why letting your money grow longer can make such a dramatic difference.

Different life events require different horizons and strategies. If you're saving for a house in just a few years, it makes sense to keep the money safe and stable. If you're building a college fund for a newborn, time is on your side — a stock fund or a 529 plan might give your investments room to grow. For a teenager's college fund, you'll lean toward safer, more stable options because there's less time to recover from downturns.

As your goals and timelines shift, update your investment strategies. For instance, as retirement nears, move some funds from stocks to more stable vehicles like bonds or cash, reducing risk as your need for the money grows closer. Periodically review your goals to confirm your investments still fit your needs and update your plans as your life changes.

Now that you have learned how to create a clear budget, build an emergency fund, manage debt wisely, and align your investment choices with your goals and time frames, you are equipped to lay a strong foundation for your financial future. These steps help transform money management from a source of stress into a tool for growth and security. By mastering these basics, you can confidently begin investing with a plan tailored to your needs, protecting yourself from unexpected setbacks while steadily working toward the life you want. As you move forward, remember that small, consistent actions add up over time — setting you on a path to financial success and peace of mind.

THREE
MEET THE ASSETS – WHAT YOU CAN INVEST IN

Have you ever wondered what exactly you're investing in when you put your money into stocks, bonds, or real estate? Many people hear these terms and feel unsure about how they actually work or why they matter. It can be confusing to know where to start or how to build a portfolio that balances growth and safety. What does it mean to own a piece of a company, lend money to the government, or invest in digital currencies? Why do some options offer steady income while others promise bigger rewards but come with more risk?

Understanding the different types of assets available is key to making smart investment choices. This chapter will introduce you to the main categories of investments and explain how each one functions, their roles, and how they fit together to help you reach your financial goals. Whether you're saving for retirement, a home, or simply want to grow your wealth steadily, knowing what you can invest in sets the foundation for success.

TRADITIONAL INVESTMENT VEHICLES: STOCKS, BONDS, MUTUAL FUNDS, INDEX FUNDS, AND ETFS

Buying a share of stock is like owning a small piece of a company. If you buy one share of Apple, you truly own part of it. Stocks represent ownership, and companies sell these shares to raise money. When people talk about "the stock market," they're talking about all the shares from thousands of companies traded each day. Investors can choose stocks from renowned brands like Nike, Microsoft, or Starbucks.

Stocks make money in two ways: if the company pays a part of its profits to shareholders, called dividends, or if the stock's price rises and you sell it for more than you paid. For example, if you buy a share of a retailer like Walmart for $100 and sell it later for $120, you make a $20 profit. Dividends are usually paid out every three months. Some companies don't pay dividends and instead reinvest profits to grow the business, which can also make the stock price increase.

Owning stocks means taking more risk. If a company does poorly, the value of your stock can drop. Markets can swing, and occasionally a company's stock price falls even when it's doing everything right. The stock market as a whole can move up or down quickly, so stocks are best for people who can leave their money invested for at least five to ten years and handle ups and downs.

You don't need a fortune to buy stocks. Many online brokers let people start with as little as $10 or $25. Some even sell "fractional shares," which means you can buy part of a share if the price is high. Stocks are bought and sold on stock exchanges such as the New York Stock Exchange (NYSE) or Nasdaq, usually through an online account.

Stocks are popular with people who want their money to grow over time. Historically, U.S. stocks have returned about 7% per year after inflation, but this isn't guaranteed every year. Some years see strong gains; others see losses.

Buying a bond is like lending your money to a company or government. When you own a bond, you are the bank. In return, the borrower promises to pay you back later — the date is called "maturity" — and sends you interest payments along the way. Bonds are safer than stocks for most investors, but no investment is completely safe.

Governments, cities, and businesses all sell bonds. The U.S. government issues **Treasury bonds**, which are considered very safe. Companies sell **corporate bonds** to fund projects, and cities offer **municipal bonds** to finance things like schools or infrastructure. Each type carries a different level of risk, but all share one feature: they pay regular interest, usually every six months.

Bonds generate returns in two ways: through interest payments and by selling the bond for more than you paid. Most investors hold bonds for the steady income. Yields vary over time: U.S. Treasury bonds might pay 2–4% annually, while riskier bonds often pay higher rates. The main risks are that the borrower might default or that rising interest rates could reduce your bond's resale value before it matures.

Bonds typically require higher minimum investments, sometimes $1,000 or more. You can buy them through brokers or directly from the issuer, such as on the U.S. Treasury's website. Bonds are a solid choice if you want greater stability and a predictable income stream.

A **mutual fund** is like a shopping cart full of investments. Instead of choosing a single stock or bond, you buy a share of a mutual fund, and a professional manager selects dozens or even hundreds of investments for you. The fund gathers money from many investors, pools it, and buys assets according to its stated goals.

There are mutual funds that focus on growth (seeking stocks that may rise quickly), income (choosing bonds or dividend-paying stocks), and balanced funds (mixing stocks and bonds for a smoother ride). For example, a growth fund might own shares of Google, Netflix, and Amazon, while an income fund might buy government and corporate bonds.

Mutual funds make money from the same sources as stocks and bonds: rising prices, dividends, and interest. Some require $500, $1,000, or even less as a minimum investment, making them accessible for beginners. They're bought directly from mutual fund companies or through online brokers.

A common myth is that mutual funds are just for experts. In fact, they're a simple way for everyday people to spread out risk and let someone else handle day-to-day decisions. Beginners often like mutual funds because they can get a diversified mix with one purchase.

Stocks have more growth potential but more risk. Bonds are steadier but don't grow as fast. Due to their diversification, mutual funds help lower the risk associated with single investments. By mixing stocks, bonds, and mutual funds, an investor gets both growth and some safety, which is the foundation of a strong investment plan.

These three tools each play an important role, and together, they help people work toward goals like buying a home, sending kids to college, or building retirement savings. Holding stocks for several years can yield significant rewards, while bonds provide stability, and mutual funds simplify investing for all investors. As mutual funds package investments together, they lead naturally to even more efficient options across markets, setting the stage for exploring index funds and exchange-traded funds, which make broad diversification and low costs possible for all investors.

REAL ESTATE & REITS: PROPERTY INVESTMENTS FOR EVERY INVESTOR

Real estate investing means putting your money into property to earn a return, either through rental income, property value growth, or both. There are different ways to get involved with real estate, from buying a house or an apartment directly to investing in pooled funds such as Real Estate Investment Trusts (REITs). Each approach has its own benefits, risks, and requirements.

Investing directly by owning property is the most traditional way to invest in real estate. You can buy residential homes, like single-family houses, or commercial buildings, like office spaces and stores. In residential rentals, you can often get started with a 20% down payment on a mortgage. For example, if you buy a $200,000 home, a down payment might be $40,000 plus closing costs. Once you own the property, you can rent it out and collect monthly payments. Suppose your mortgage, taxes, and maintenance cost $1,100 per month, but you rent the home for $1,400 per month. That gives you $300 per month in passive income, before occasional repair costs or vacancies. Over time, the property may also rise in value — a concept known as appreciation. If your $200,000 house grows to $250,000 over ten years, that's a $50,000 gain when you sell, not counting transaction costs.

Direct ownership has clear risks. Tenants can miss payments or damage the property. The house could sit empty between renters, adding stress or lost income. You'll be responsible for repairs, paying property taxes, and dealing with issues like leaky roofs or broken appliances. These property management tasks require involvement or the hiring of a property manager, which comes with additional fees. Selling a house takes time, so real estate is not as straightforward to cash out of as stocks or bonds.

REITs provide a way to invest in real estate without owning a building yourself. REITs are companies that buy, manage, or finance real estate and trade on stock markets like regular shares. You might invest as little as $1,000 in a publicly traded REIT through a brokerage account. Your money joins that of thousands of other investors, and the REIT uses it to buy things like shopping malls, hospitals, or apartment complexes. You receive dividends, typically paid every quarter, from the rental income and profits generated by these properties. For instance, if you invest $1,000 in a REIT yielding 5%, you'd expect about $50 per year in payouts, though this is not guaranteed and depends on real estate market health.

REITs are popular because of their liquidity. You can buy and sell shares easily, unlike selling a property. However, because they trade on public stock markets, REIT prices can fluctuate quickly, exposing you to market swings. REIT income is often taxed as ordinary income, not at the lower long-term capital gains rate, so tax planning is important.

Some investors look into real estate crowdfunding platforms. These websites let multiple investors pool small amounts — often $500–$1,000 — into a single project. You might help finance a new apartment complex or hotel, sharing in rental income or project profits. Crowdfunding lets you invest smaller amounts and diversify across several projects. But it often comes with less liquidity than REITs, as your money could be locked up for several years until the project finishes or sells. These deals generally require less day-to-day involvement but carry higher risks if the project fails.

Real estate mutual funds offer another way to diversify. These funds invest in a mix of REITs or real estate-related companies. With as little as $250, you can spread risk over a wide range of properties, and professionals will manage the investments. Liquidity is high, but like REITs, market swings can affect values.

The main benefits of real estate are steady income, possible price growth, and low correlation with stocks and bonds, which can protect your portfolio during stock market downturns. Many investors appreciate getting monthly cash flow from rentals or quarterly dividends from REITs. But real estate is usually more complex than stocks or bonds and has unique risks, such as property damage or real estate market cycles that affect values. Economic downturns can mean falling property prices and lower rent collections.

Practical risk management helps. For direct ownership, keeping a cash reserve covers repairs and vacancies. For REITs or funds, diversification across different property types lessens risk. Understanding local real estate trends and not overpaying for a property are key to long-term success.

This blend of income, appreciation, and diversification makes real estate a useful part of an investment portfolio. With options from hands-on property to easy-access REITs, even small investors can take advantage of opportunities in the real estate market.

CRYPTOCURRENCY: DIGITAL INVESTING FOR BEGINNERS

Digital money is something most people already use every day, whether it's paying with a bank card or sending funds through an app. Cryptocurrency works like digital money too, but it is different because it doesn't rely on banks or governments. Instead, it uses secure technology called blockchain, which is like a digital ledger or notebook everyone can see, but no one can change without others seeing it too. Each cryptocurrency, like Bitcoin or Ethereum, runs on its version of this ledger.

Cryptocurrency, often just called "crypto," is a type of digital asset. It is created and stored electronically. The most well-known example is Bitcoin, started in 2009. Bitcoin's idea was to allow people to send money over the internet, directly from one person to another, without a bank in between. Others soon followed, such as Ethereum, which does something similar to Bitcoin but also lets people make agreements, or "smart contracts," right in the code.

How Cryptocurrency Works: The Basics

Think of each Bitcoin as a special token that lives on its online ledger. If you "own" a Bitcoin, the ledger records that your digital wallet controls it. When you send Bitcoin to someone, imagine moving a digital token from your wallet to theirs. This transaction is recorded with many others, forming a secure and permanent log. Millions of computers worldwide keep copies of this log, known as the blockchain, making it very hard for anyone to cheat or change history.

Ethereum works in a similar way, but it's not just about sending tokens. People can write rules called smart contracts — little programs that live on the Ethereum blockchain. These rules can automatically move Ethereum tokens between users once certain conditions are met, much like a digital vending machine that only releases a soda after you put in the right amount of money.

Why People Invest in Cryptocurrency

A few factors make cryptocurrency attractive to investors:

- **Potential for Big Returns:** Bitcoin, for example, was once almost worthless and later reached values in the tens of thousands of dollars per coin. This potential has drawn many investors hoping for high profits.
- **Limited Supply:** Bitcoin has a built-in rule: only about 21 million will ever exist. Some other cryptocurrencies have similar limits, which can make them seem scarce and possibly more valuable.
- **New Technology:** Other applications of the blockchain technology, which powers cryptocurrencies, include tracking supply chains, recording property ownership, and storing medical records. Some investors see this as a sign that these systems have staying power.

Common Concerns and Myths

Many newcomers worry that cryptocurrency is only for tech experts or criminals. In reality, anyone can buy and use cryptocurrency with a little guidance. Another myth is that it is completely anonymous — every transaction is actually recorded on the public blockchain, though identities are hidden behind wallet addresses.

Some people also think cryptocurrencies are "get rich quick" schemes. While some have made a lot of money, prices often swing wildly, and there are no guarantees of profit. Unlike stocks or real estate, cryptocurrencies don't have underlying companies or physical assets, which makes prices hard to predict.

Getting Started: Buying, Storing, and Trading Safely

1. **Choose a Reputable Exchange:** Websites like Coinbase, Kraken, or Binance let you buy and sell Bitcoin, Ethereum, and other digital coins. These exchanges require you to create an account, verify your identity, and link a bank account.

2. **Store Your Crypto Securely:** You can leave your coins on the exchange (online wallet), but for higher safety, move them to your own "wallet." There are two main wallet types:

Method	Description	Security Level
Hot Wallet	Online app or website	Moderate
Cold Wallet	Hardware device, disconnected from web	High

Cold wallets, like USB sticks, protect your coins from online hacks.

3. **Protect Your Information:** Use strong passwords. Turn on two-factor authentication (2FA), which requires a code sent to your phone or an app before logging in. Never share your private keys (the secret codes that control your coins).

Building Cryptocurrency into a Portfolio

Cryptocurrencies are riskier than traditional investments. Most experts suggest new investors keep crypto to a small slice of their overall portfolio. A common recommendation is 1-5% of your investments. This way, if prices drop sharply, your losses won't overwhelm your finances, but if values rise, you still benefit.

It's important to research before buying any coin. Look for facts: what problems does the cryptocurrency try to solve, who is running the project, and how many coins will exist? Reliable information can be found on official project websites and trusted investment sites.

Risks and Rewards

Crypto values can change dramatically in a short time. Values might be driven by news, government decisions, or changes to the technology itself. For example, a government ban or a major hack can cause prices to crash. On the other hand, adoption by big companies or positive technical updates can send values soaring.

In the long term, some investors see cryptocurrency as a way to balance other types of investments, like stocks or bonds. With careful research, safe habits, and realistic expectations, cryptocurrency can play a role in a modern investment plan, as long as you manage your risks wisely.

Now that you understand the key investment options — stocks, bonds, mutual funds, real estate, and cryptocurrency — you're better equipped to start building a balanced portfolio that fits your goals and comfort with risk. Each asset class offers unique benefits and challenges, and combining them thoughtfully can help protect your money while aiming for growth over time. Whether you choose to invest directly or through funds, begin small, stay informed, and remember that investing is a journey best approached with patience and clear purpose. With this foundation, you're ready to explore strategies that make your money work harder for you and move confidently toward your financial future.

FOUR
THE POWER OF DIVERSIFICATION

Have you ever felt uneasy about putting all your money into a single investment, only to watch its value drop unexpectedly? Maybe you've heard stories of friends who rushed to buy the latest hot stock and ended up losing most of what they put in. It's natural to wonder if there's a safer way to invest — one that doesn't depend on guessing which asset will perform best or avoiding sudden losses.

Investing can feel overwhelming, especially when markets shift without warning and the future seems uncertain. People new to investing often worry about risk and how to protect their hard-earned money while still aiming for growth. Understanding how to spread your investments thoughtfully can ease some of this anxiety and help build confidence. This chapter explores why diversifying your investments is an essential strategy to manage risk and work toward steady returns. We'll look at how spreading money across different types of assets can create balance, reduce surprises, and support your financial goals over time.

UNDERSTANDING DIVERSIFICATION AND ASSET ALLOCATION

Imagine holding a basket full of eggs while walking down a bumpy path. If you stumble and all your eggs are in that one basket, every single egg might break. But if you split them between several sturdy baskets, a single slip may only cost you a few. This simple idea perfectly illustrates diversification in investing. Diversification means spreading your money across different types of investments instead of putting it all in one place. The goal is to reduce the risk of losing everything if one investment performs poorly.

Many beginners think investing is about picking one winning stock or following the latest hot tip. While these approaches can sometimes work, they also carry significant risk. Diversification offers a proven way to manage that risk by reducing the impact of any single investment that underperforms. Consider an investor who puts all their savings into one technology company. If that company struggles, their financial future is in danger. By contrast, someone who invests in a mix of technology, healthcare, real estate, and bonds is less likely to lose everything, even if one sector has a difficult year.

History provides many examples of the power of diversification. During the tech bubble of the early 2000s, investors who held only technology stocks saw their savings vanish. Those who also owned other investments, such as bonds or non-tech stocks, avoided the worst losses. Diversification acts like a shock absorber. When one part of the market declines, others may hold steady or even rise, softening the impact.

The benefits of diversification go beyond just avoiding big losses. Diversification addresses one major area of risk. By investing in different things that don't always move together in price, you lower the chance that all your investments will lose value at the same time. This creates the potential for more steady, reliable returns over time. Imagine a portfolio with stocks, bonds, and some real estate. If the stock market plunges, bond prices might rise as investors seek safety, and real estate values might remain stable or change slowly. The different pieces work together to balance out gains and losses.

Market ups and downs are a natural part of investing. Diversification helps cushion against market volatility, the sudden changes in prices that can be unsettling for investors. Imagine a new investor during a market downturn. If their portfolio includes many types of assets, they're less likely to panic when one part drops in value. Industry-specific events, like a scandal at a large oil company or new technology disrupting an old business model, are as well less threatening when your investments are spread across various sectors. This approach doesn't remove all risk, but it helps reduce surprises.

There are a few myths about diversification that can make beginners hesitate. Some people think only the rich can afford to diversify, but today, anyone can do it. Many apps and investment products let you invest small amounts across different assets. Others believe diversification is too complex, requiring profound knowledge or expert help. While investing can be complicated, the basics of diversification are straightforward and easy to put into practice. Some assume you have to know a lot about global markets. In reality, even beginners can diversify by investing in index funds or exchange-traded funds (ETFs), which already contain a variety of companies, industries, or even countries.

Diversification looks different depending on what you invest in. Spreading your money between stocks, which represent ownership in companies, and bonds, which are loans to companies or governments, is a beneficial starting point. You can also include real estate through real estate investment trusts (REITs), which allow you to invest in property without buying buildings yourself. Adding international investments broadens your reach and helps protect against problems in any single country. Diversifying by industry and by the size of companies — mixing large, stable firms with smaller, growing ones — offers more layers of protection.

Thinking about risk is important for investors. There are two main kinds: systematic risk and unsystematic risk. Systematic risk affects the whole market, like a global recession or a sudden rise in interest rates — no amount of diversification can avoid it completely. Unsystematic risk, however, is tied to specific companies or industries.

Diversification is a powerful tool for lowering unsystematic risk. By diversifying your investments, setbacks in one area are less likely to harm you. The end result is risk-adjusted returns, meaning you're putting yourself in a position to earn rewards that make sense for your level of risk.

Diversification matters because it offers protection, steadier growth, and a more confident path toward your goals. You don't need to be wealthy or an expert. All it takes is the willingness to spread your investments broadly and let time — and the power of diversification — work in your favor.

SAMPLE PORTFOLIOS FOR EVERY INVESTOR

Many investors wonder how to turn the theory of diversification into a plan they can actually use. By looking at sample portfolios for different goals, it's possible to see how different asset mixes cater to varying levels of risk, time horizons, and life stages. Let's explore three portfolio types — the conservative, the balanced, and the growth-oriented — and see how each one works in the real world.

A conservative portfolio centers around stability and capital preservation. The main aim is to minimize losses, even if it means lower returns. Imagine an investor with $10,000 whose main goal is to preserve capital for a near-term need, like a home down payment or retirement in a few years. The allocation might look like:

Asset Class	Percentage	Dollar Amount
Government Bonds	50%	$5,000
High-Grade Corporate Bonds	20%	$2,000
Dividend-Paying Stocks	15%	$1,500
Broad Market Index Fund (ETF)	10%	$1,000
Cash or Money Market	5%	$500

Most of the portfolio lies in government and high-quality corporate bonds. These tend to offer safety in tough times and generate predictable income. Dividend-paying stocks provide modest growth and regular cash flow, acting as a cushion when the market stumbles. A broad market ETF captures a slice of the equity market, but at a small enough portion that it won't cause big waves when stocks swing. Keeping a cash buffer lets the investor cover unexpected needs without selling investments at a difficult time. Someone choosing this model usually has a low risk tolerance, a shorter time frame, or may be managing funds for a big purchase within three to five years. They value peace of mind over chasing after higher returns. This portfolio may not grow as quickly as others in volatile markets, but it rarely falls behind — even when stocks decline sharply, bonds and cash cushion the impact.

A balanced portfolio aims for moderate growth but adds a reasonable degree of safety. This approach blends stocks and bonds to balance out risk and return. Suppose a person plans to invest $10,000 for 10 years, such as saving for a child's college education or a future house. Their allocation might be:

Asset Class	Percentage	Dollar Amount
U.S. Stocks (ETF or mutual fund)	35%	$3,500
International Stocks	15%	$1,500
Bonds (mix of U.S. Treasuries and corporates)	40%	$4,000
Real Estate Investment Trust (REIT ETF)	5%	$500
Cash/Short-Term Instruments	5%	$500

About half the portfolio stays in bonds and cash, limiting downside during downturns. Adding both U.S. and international stocks enables participation in market growth from different regions, spreading risk. REITs bring extra diversification because real estate often moves differently from stocks or bonds. This arrangement typically serves investors who are midway in their careers or have longer-term ambitions, like building wealth for retirement over a decade or more. While this portfolio can decline in a rough market, its blend of assets helps it recover and smooths out wild swings. The result is an evenhanded approach — higher potential than a conservative model, but enough defense to avoid sleepless nights during market turbulence.

Seeking the largest possible gains means building a growth-oriented portfolio. With bigger risk comes the potential for bigger reward — and a sturdier stomach for market ups and downs. Suppose a younger investor in their 20s or 30s is putting $10,000 to work for retirement that's decades away. Their mix might look like:

Asset Class	Percentage	Dollar Amount
U.S. Stocks (ETF or mutual fund)	45%	$4,500
International Stocks	25%	$2,500
Small Cap & Emerging Market Stocks	15%	$1,500
Sector ETFs (e.g., tech, healthcare)	10%	$1,000
Bonds/Cash	5%	$500

Here, stocks dominate. The focus is on high-growth options — U.S. and international, plus a slice in small-company and emerging-market stocks for more adventurous upside. Adding sector funds increases the chance for above-average returns if certain industries surge. Bonds and cash form a tiny buffer for emergencies. Because the goal is decades away, short-term losses are less worrying, and there's time to recover from downturns. This model supports long-term wealth building and is ideal for someone with plenty of time, a higher risk tolerance, and no immediate need for the money. In good years, the growth portfolio can race ahead, but it will also swing wider than the others during downturns.

Each of these portfolios demonstrates practical diversification. By blending asset types, regions, and even market segments, they spread out risk and position for suitable returns. These models are not strict rules — they offer templates that can be tweaked based on personal priorities, financial goals, and stage of life. The right mix helps investors face uncertainty with confidence and the optimism that comes from a smart, diversified plan.

MASTERING REBALANCING TECHNIQUES

A well-constructed portfolio needs regular maintenance to stay on track and achieve its goals. Even if all the right choices are made in the beginning — spreading investments between stocks, bonds, and other assets — real-world changes will shift how much each asset makes up in the portfolio. Over time, those shifts can turn a balanced portfolio into one with more risk than intended or with too little growth potential. The simple act of rebalancing means checking and correcting the mix so it matches the plan. Certain signals let investors know when it's time to rebalance.

Time-based triggers are among the most common. Many investors set a schedule to rebalance their portfolios at regular intervals, such as quarterly or annually. The idea is that regardless of what the market does, a check-in happens at set times. This method makes portfolio management part of a routine, so busy periods or market excitement do not cause it to be forgotten. Still, a lot can happen between those calendar dates, so some people use percentage-based triggers instead. This approach sets a rule like "If any asset class moves more than 5% away from its target allocation, it's time to act." For example, if a portfolio is designed to be 60% stocks and 40% bonds, and rising stock prices raise stocks to 68%, that's an 8% drift — enough to trigger a rebalance. Life events also sometimes call for a change. Getting married, receiving an inheritance, or planning for retirement can all mean a portfolio should be rebalanced based on new goals, financial situations, or risk tolerance.

Breaking down the rebalancing process makes it less daunting. The first step is to assess the current allocation. This involves listing each asset and its current value, then calculating the percentage that each one represents in the overall portfolio. For instance, in a $10,000 portfolio where $6,800 is in stocks and $3,200 is in bonds, stocks now make up 68% of the portfolio rather than the intended 60%. The second step is to identify which assets need adjustment. The aim is to bring the allocation back in line with the targets, so it's clear whether to trim some investments or add to others. Finally, make strategic buying and selling decisions. If stocks have grown beyond their target, some are sold and the proceeds are used to buy other assets that have fallen behind, like bonds.

A real-life example makes this clearer. Consider a portfolio designed with 60% stocks ($6,000) and 40% bonds ($4,000). After a year, the stock market has performed well, and stocks are now worth $7,200, while bonds have grown to $4,200. The new total is $11,400. To see whether rebalancing is needed, calculate the new percentages:

Asset	Current Value	Portfolio %	Target %
Stocks	$7,200	63.2%	60%
Bonds	$4,200	36.8%	40%

Stocks have drifted up by 3.2%, while bonds are now underweight. To restore the target balance, calculate 60% of $11,400 = $6,840 for stocks and 40% of $11,400 = $4,560 for bonds. This means the investor should sell $360 from stocks ($7,200 - $6,840) and use that money to buy bonds, bringing the portfolio back to its original ratio.

Many investors notice challenges when rebalancing. Taxes can come into play if selling certain assets triggers capital gains, which may result in a tax bill. Transaction costs — small fees for buying or selling investments — can add up, especially in smaller accounts, so it's wise to check if the costs outweigh the benefits. Emotional barriers often arise, too, since it feels counterintuitive to sell assets that are performing well and buy those that are lagging. However, rebalancing is necessary because otherwise, market swings could throw the portfolio off course. Worry about market timing can also creep in, since no one wants to buy high or sell low. Sticking to a set schedule or clear rules helps remove guesswork and emotion from the process.

Staying organized makes rebalancing easier. Many brokerages and investment platforms offer tools that show a current asset allocation at a glance and automatically highlight when balances stray from targets.

Some apps and spreadsheet templates let users track their progress, sending reminders or generating easy-to-understand charts. A simple worksheet where investors log each asset, its value, and its percentage of the portfolio can be helpful, especially for those who want a hands-on approach. These resources save time and mean there's less risk of missing important signals.

Regular rebalancing keeps portfolios healthy, on purpose, and less swayed by emotion or sudden market moves. Consistent habits and the right tools help investors stick to their plans and manage risk while aiming for long-term growth.

Now that you understand how diversification spreads risk and how rebalancing keeps your investments aligned with your goals, you're better equipped to build a portfolio that grows steadily and weathers market ups and downs. By mixing different asset types and regularly reviewing your allocation, you can protect yourself from sudden losses while aiming for returns that match your comfort with risk. This approach is not just for experts or the wealthy — anyone can start small and grow smarter over time. With these tools in hand, you're ready to take confident, thoughtful steps toward a secure financial future.

FIVE
GETTING STARTED – YOUR FIRST INVESTMENTS

Have you ever felt overwhelmed by the many choices and steps involved in starting to invest your money? Maybe you've glanced at investment apps or heard stories about people growing their wealth through the stock market, but the details often seem confusing or intimidating. Questions like "Which platform should I trust?" or "How much money do I need to get started?" might be holding you back from taking that first step.

Starting with investing can feel daunting because there are so many options and considerations. From picking the right brokerage to understanding account types and managing deposits, it's easy to feel unsure about where to begin. This chapter will guide you through these early decisions and actions, helping you gain clarity and confidence as you open your first investment account, make your initial investments, and set up a plan that keeps your money working for you over time.

SELECTING YOUR BROKERAGE OR INVESTMENT PLATFORM

Many first-time investors feel unsure where to begin, faced with a maze of platforms and brokerages promising everything from low fees to cutting-edge technology. Understanding the differences between traditional brokerages, online investment platforms, and mobile-first apps will help you make a confident start.

Traditional brokerages often have long-established reputations, offering personal advisors and physical branches. These can be valuable for those who appreciate one-on-one support and are willing to pay for more comprehensive service. The rise of online platforms and mobile-first apps, however, has made investing far more accessible. Online platforms typically provide web-based dashboards, educational tools, and digital support systems at lower costs. Mobile-first apps, designed primarily for smartphones, feature simple interfaces and instant notifications that appeal to younger, tech-savvy investors who value speed and convenience.

When choosing where to begin, focus on the features that matter most to beginners. Start with the user interface: a clean, intuitive layout helps prevent mistakes when placing trades or checking your portfolio. Platforms like Robinhood and Wealthsimple stand out for their straightforward design and ease of navigation. Educational resources are equally important. Look for beginner guides, glossaries, tutorials, and in-app quizzes that builds your understanding step by step. Fidelity and Vanguard, for instance, are known for their comprehensive learning centers and interactive tools. Finally, strong customer support can make all the difference when you need help. Check whether live chat, phone assistance, or community forums are available, and how quickly you can expect a response.

Fee structures are an important part of the decision. The move toward commission-free trading — where buying and selling stocks or ETFs no longer incurs a per-trade charge — has changed the landscape, making investing more affordable than ever. Robinhood, E*TRADE, and SoFi Invest have adopted this fee model. However, pay special attention to account minimums and maintenance fees. Some platforms require a set amount to open an account (for example, Vanguard traditionally required $1,000 for some mutual funds), while others allow you to begin with just a few dollars. Ongoing maintenance or inactivity fees can eat into profits, especially for those who aren't planning frequent trades.

Security is non-negotiable. Look for two-factor authentication, SIPC or FDIC insurance in the United States, or similar protections elsewhere, and transparent data encryption policies. Reputable platforms will display their regulatory compliance and explain how your assets are protected. Global investors can access research platforms from their respective countries. Interactive Brokers and Saxo Bank, for instance, are popular internationally and support multiple currencies and languages, making them ideal for those outside the U.S. or for users interested in international markets.

The types of investment products a platform offers can shape your long-term strategy. Some platforms specialize in stocks and exchange-traded funds (ETFs), appealing to those who want instant access to fast-moving markets. Mutual funds, available on Fidelity, Charles Schwab, and Vanguard, work well for those seeking diversified, managed portfolios. Newer apps like Acorns or Stash offer automatic investing through "round-ups" or curated portfolios, catering to users who want a passive, set-and-forget approach.

Practical Tools for Choosing an Investment Platform

A structured comparison can clarify your options. Use the table below to evaluate platforms side-by-side:

Feature	Platform A	Platform B	Platform C
User Interface	Clear/Simple	Complex	Modern
Educational Resources	Extensive	Limited	Moderate
Fees/Commissions	Low/Free	High	Free
Account Minimums	None	$500	None
Investment Products	ETFs/Stocks	Mutual Funds	All types
Global Access	Yes	No	Yes
Security	Strong	Standard	Strong

Ask yourself:

- Am I comfortable navigating the app or website without confusion?
- Does the platform offer the educational help and customer service I need?
- What fees and minimums apply, and do they fit my budget?
- What kind of investments do I want to start with?
- Is this platform usable and legal in my country?

Watch out for red flags such as unlisted fees, poor customer reviews, weak security statements, or platforms lacking regulatory oversight. Examples like Robinhood appeal to those wanting no commissions and a mobile interface, while Schwab attracts with a broad product list, educational breadth, and robust customer care. Acorns is suitable for anyone looking to invest spare change with minimal effort.

Choosing the right platform comes down to aligning features with your strategy, support needs, and investment products. Some investors need constant support and robust educational resources, while others value low fees and global accessibility. As you narrow your choices, prepare to gather the necessary documents and meet any account requirements to open your first investment account smoothly in the next stage.

OPENING AN ACCOUNT AND MAKING YOUR FIRST INVESTMENT

Choosing the right investment platform marks the beginning of your journey, but opening and funding your account is where plans start to become reality. Opening an account typically starts with an online form. Most platforms ask for your name, contact details, Social Security number, and employment information. This may feel personal, but it's a legal requirement to protect your account and comply with regulations. Expect to provide a clear copy or photo of a government-issued ID, like a driver's license or passport, to verify your identity. If you're setting up an IRA or other specialized account, you may also be asked for additional documentation, such as a beneficiary designation or evidence of current employment status.

Several account types are usually available for investing. The standard option is an individual brokerage account. This account works well for most beginners and is suitable if you simply want to buy and sell investments on your timeline. Some platforms offer joint accounts for couples or partners. Retirement accounts, like Traditional or Roth IRAs, come with tax advantages but also have stricter rules about deposits and withdrawals. Custodial accounts let parents invest on behalf of their children, while trust accounts serve more specialized needs. Each option is clearly labeled during the sign-up process, but it helps to know what fits your goals before moving forward.

Platforms often require an initial deposit to activate your account. Some well-known brokers, like Fidelity or Charles Schwab, let you start with no minimum — technically, you could open and leave the account unfunded for a while. Others, such as Vanguard, may require a $1,000 minimum for certain accounts. For beginners, starting with an initial deposit of $100–$500 is both manageable and meaningful, providing enough funds to explore basic investments without feeling overwhelmed.

Once your account is open, funding methods vary. Bank transfers (ACH), wire transfers, and checks are common, while some platforms now support PayPal or even debit cards. The default option is often bank transfer, where you securely link your checking or savings account to the investment platform. Linking your bank is straightforward: you enter your bank's routing and account numbers or log into your online banking through a secure connection provided by the platform. Many applications use encrypted integrations with major banks, so your login details are never stored. Bank transfers tend to be free and usually take one to three business days to process. Wire transfers might move money within the same day but often cost $15–$25 per transaction.

Typical Processing Times and What to Expect

After confirming your funding method, you'll usually see a pending deposit in your investment account within 24–72 hours. Most platforms clearly display the status of your transfer — look for messages like "deposit in progress" or "awaiting funds." Funds are often available for investing after the transaction settles, though some platforms offer instant deposit features for small amounts (e.g., up to $1,000 immediately) if you're using a linked bank account. Larger transfers, wires, or paper checks may require full clearing, extending the wait by a couple of business days.

Navigating Security Measures and Verification Steps

Security is a common concern for first-time investors. Most platforms require two-step verification — after entering your password, you'll be sent a code by email or text to confirm your identity. Some may ask security questions or use facial recognition if you're applying via mobile app. Account verification helps prevent fraud and unauthorized access. It's also normal to be asked for a selfie holding your ID or to answer a few quick questions from your credit history.

If paperwork is missing or a document image is blurry, expect a quick request for a re-upload, with clear instructions on what's needed.

Managing Obstacles and Making Funding Easier

Occasional snags are common. Banks may reject a link if your name doesn't match exactly, or a deposit may be held up if your account information is mistyped. Double-check details, use name formatting that matches your bank records, and keep funding amounts within daily limits to avoid holds. If your platform offers a test deposit — typically two tiny amounts under $1 — that's to confirm the account is yours. Enter those exact amounts when prompted to activate your link.

Recurring deposits are a helpful feature for building good habits. Most platforms let you set automatic transfers from your bank for a set amount on a weekly or monthly schedule. Starting with $25 or $50 per month makes investing routine and less intimidating, ensuring steady growth over time.

Once your deposit clears, your account will show available cash. You're now ready to purchase investments — from stocks to index funds. Some platforms offer instant investing with settled funds, while others may display a "settlement period" for new deposits. Watch for confirmation emails with details, and keep records of your transfer receipts for quick reference. Starting small makes the process less stressful, keeps risk low, and helps you build confidence before making larger investments.

AUTOMATING YOUR INVESTMENTS FOR LONG-TERM GROWTH

Automatic investing is a system where money leaves your bank account and moves into your investment account according to a schedule you set. Automatic investing puts your wealth-building plan on autopilot, eliminating the need to decide every month how much to invest — or worse, to forget to invest entirely. Your money works for you in the background, quietly growing without the need for daily attention or energy.

Setting up automatic investing has several valuable benefits, especially for people who feel busy, anxious, or overwhelmed by the idea of investing. First, automation removes emotion from the process. On tough days when spending might feel tempting, the money is already on its way to your investments. This approach prevents emotional decisions and keeps your strategy on track. Second, automatic investing helps build financial discipline. Regular contributions, no matter how small, turn into a steady habit that pays off over time. Third, it saves time and mental bandwidth, because there's no need to remember, calculate, or manually transfer money each time you want to invest. Finally, setting up a recurring investment plan takes advantage of the principle of dollar-cost averaging: by investing consistently, you spread your money over different market conditions instead of trying to time the market.

Most investment platforms and brokerage firms have built-in tools to help you automate your investments. Once you decide how much you want to invest and how often, you provide your bank account details and set the schedule. For example, popular apps like Fidelity, Vanguard, Robinhood, or Acorns let you choose an amount — say, $50, $100, or $200 — and pick how frequently you want that amount invested. The platform then moves your chosen money on your preferred schedule, either buying shares directly or adding to your account's balance for investment.

Common Automatic Investment Schedules

Frequency	Minimum Example	Typical User
Weekly	$25	Freelancers/gig workers, people with weekly paychecks
Bi-weekly	$50	Salary earners paid every other week
Monthly	$100	Most common for people with steady monthly income

If you get paid every Friday, you might set aside $25 to invest at the end of each week. This means you're investing $100 each month, which can add up to more than $1,200 a year. Someone with a biweekly paycheck could invest $50 every two weeks, matching deposits with pay periods to make managing cash flow easier. Monthly schedules are good for planning investments around rent and bills, which are due at the same time each month.

It's normal to have concerns about giving up manual control. People often ask, "What if my income sometimes drops?" or "What happens if I can't afford the scheduled investment one month?" The best automatic systems are flexible. Most platforms allow you to pause, lower, or adjust your deposit anytime. You can start small with as little as $10 or $25. Over time, as you see your balance grow and your confidence increases, you'll find it easier to bump up the amount.

To figure out what an appropriate automated amount looks like, start by listing out your repeating monthly expenses. Subtract your rent, utilities, groceries, and other necessities from your typical monthly income. The leftover is your pool for savings and investing. Choose a percentage or dollar amount that feels comfortable — sometimes that means starting with $25 or $50 a month. If you have an irregular or gig-based income, consider setting your automation to a lower base threshold, such as $10 weekly, then topping off manually at the end of a strong month.

Here's how this plays out in real life: Mia earns about $2,800 a month after taxes, with variable freelance jobs. She lists $2,100 worth of bills and essentials. That leaves $700 for savings, but with unpredictable months, she picks a safe amount of $25 per week, which works out to $100 per month automatically invested. In months with more gigs, she manually adds extra hours to her schedule.

Visualizing the Power of Compounding

Let's compare three automatic schedules for a $50 monthly investment at a 6% annual return over 10 years:

Frequency	Annual Total Invested	Est. 10-Year Value*
Monthly	$600	~$8,200
Bi-weekly	$1,300	~$17,600
Weekly	$2,600	~$35,200

*Assumes all contributions are invested regularly; market returns vary.

Adjusting automated investments is simple. As your income grows, update your plan every six months or after a raise. If you start at $25 per week, but next year you have a higher salary, consider increasing to $35 or $50. Even small increases accelerate long-term gains. If you ever need to pause, most platforms make it easy with just a few clicks.

Automation turns investing into a steady force for building wealth, even when life gets hectic. By picking a manageable schedule, adjusting as your situation changes, and taking advantage of technology, anyone can create a foundation for financial security that runs on autopilot.

Now that you understand how to select the right investment platform, open and fund your account, and set up automatic investing, you're well-positioned to take confident steps toward building your financial future. By choosing tools that fit your needs and automating your contributions, you simplify the process and remove many common barriers that hold beginners back. As you move forward, remember that investing is a journey — starting small, staying consistent, and adjusting your plan as life changes will help you develop habits that grow your wealth steadily over time. With these foundational steps in place, you are ready to explore more advanced strategies and watch your investments work for you, even when life gets busy.

SIX
AVOIDING COSTLY MISTAKES

Imagine sitting at your kitchen table, watching the value of your investments drop day after day. You feel a knot in your stomach as headlines scream about market crashes and economic uncertainty. Suddenly, an urge takes over — you want to sell everything before you lose more. But in the rush to act, doubts creep in: Did I just make a costly mistake? How do others seem to stay calm and come out ahead?

Many new investors face moments like this, caught between emotions and choices that can change their financial future. Fear, the pressure to follow rising trends, and the temptation to react impulsively are common obstacles that can hinder even the best-intentioned individuals. Without knowing how to recognize these traps, it's easy to make decisions that erode hard-earned gains and slow progress toward building wealth.

This chapter covers the hidden challenges investors face and reveals why understanding these pitfalls is crucial. By learning how emotional responses and overlooked costs can quietly sabotage success, you'll gain clarity on how to navigate investing with confidence and caution. Recognizing these hurdles early empowers you to build habits that protect your money and set the stage for long-term growth.

OVERCOMING EMOTIONAL TRAPS AND THE MYTH OF MARKET TIMING

Many smart investment strategies unravel not because of lack of planning, but because of powerful emotions clouding judgment. The most common emotional traps investors fall into are fear, fear of missing out (FOMO), and panic. Each of these can prompt impulsive choices that derail even the most carefully crafted investment plans. By understanding these traps, recognizing their signs, and learning strategies to stay objective, investors can increase their chances of long-term financial success.

Fear: Market Downturns and Defensive Instincts

Fear is a survival instinct that alerts us to danger, but in investing, it often prompts people to flee the market when things get rough. When markets fall sharply, such as during a major correction or recession, negative headlines and steep portfolio losses trigger anxiety. Investors confronting a 15% drop in the stock market might immediately worry: Will I lose everything if I ride this out?

This fear usually leads to actions like selling stocks at a loss or moving money to cash as a protective measure. Real-world examples include the rapid sell-off during the early days of a financial crisis or news of a sudden global event. Investors often rush to exit, hoping to avoid further losses, but this often results in them missing the subsequent recovery. Research by behavioral economists like Daniel Kahneman has shown that people are wired to feel losses more deeply than gains, leading to risk-averse behavior during downturns.

The effects of giving into fear can be severe. By selling at the bottom, investors turn paper losses into real ones, missing out on future gains when the market rebounds. To counter this, investors should ask themselves: Am I acting because of short-term fear, or does the data warrant a long-term change? Taking a pause before reacting — such as committing to a 24-hour waiting period before any major investment move — can help bring anxiety levels down. Writing down the original reasons for your investments and checking if those fundamentals have truly changed offers clarity. A simple checklist can be helpful:

Self-Check	Response Needed?
Is this decision based on headlines?	Wait 24 hours
Are fundamentals still strong?	Stay the course
Am I following my long-term strategy?	Re-evaluate only if long-term goals shift

FOMO: Urgency and Herd Mentality

The fear of missing out, or FOMO, strikes hardest during hot investment booms. News of friends making quick profits in trending assets, or seeing a stock's value skyrocket overnight, creates this urgent need to join the crowd. Technology stocks in the late 1990s or cryptocurrencies in recent years are classic cases where investors felt compelled to buy in, afraid of being left behind.

FOMO often prompts investors to abandon their regular research or carefully planned strategies. Instead, choices are driven by hype, headlines, and social proof. This can lead to buying at inflated prices, just as excitement is peaking. Inevitably, the excitement cools and prices correct, leaving latecomers with potential losses.

To manage FOMO, it helps to pause and ask: Would I still invest in this asset if it wasn't popular? Does it align with my goals and risk tolerance? Writing down your reasons for investing can clarify if the decision fits your plan or is being shaped by envy or social pressure. Many successful investors recommend having a "cooling off" period for any investments inspired by trends. If after 48 hours the rationale still makes sense and passes your criteria, it may be worth considering. Otherwise, sticking to your personal investing guidelines keeps FOMO in check.

Panic: Sudden Changes and Hasty Choices

Panic is a more intense variant of fear, often seen during dramatic market swings over a very short period. When markets crash on breaking news or unexpected events — such as a country defaulting on its debt or a pandemic emerging — logic tends to fly out the window. The urge to act quickly can overwhelm any prior planning.

Investors in panic mode might rapidly sell off assets, shift everything into cash, or abandon their strategy entirely. Panic-driven trades are usually the result of feeling completely out of control. During the 2008 financial crisis, studies on investor behavior revealed that many who liquidated their investments during the height of fear missed the substantial recovery that followed, often waiting many years to regain their former wealth.

Building emotional resilience means preparing for volatility before it happens. Creating a written investment plan, complete with rules for when and how to rebalance, sets up automatic responses that override panic. Using reminder notes like "Don't make decisions at market extremes" or setting thresholds (e.g., only reviewing portfolios quarterly, not daily) also helps. Checking in with questions such as "Am I acting out of fear or informed analysis?" puts a pause on rash decisions.

Recognizing these emotional traps and having practical steps to manage them connects directly to long-term investing success. Emotional discipline supports the steady, consistent approach that research shows delivers better returns over time. Investors who learn to spot their triggers, establish personal guardrails, and stick to their plans can ride out market ups and downs much more effectively.

IDENTIFYING HIGH FEES, HIDDEN COSTS, AND OVERTRADING

Every dollar invested should work as hard as possible for its owner, but fees and hidden expenses can quietly siphon growth from a well-designed portfolio. Even low-sounding percentages, when stretched over years and applied to large sums, can snowball into significant reductions in wealth. Understanding these costs and minimizing their effect is at the heart of smart, cost-conscious investing.

Management Fees and Expense Ratios

Investment products, whether mutual funds or exchange-traded funds (ETFs), routinely charge management fees. These fees are typically stated as a percentage of assets under management, known as the expense ratio. For example, a fund with a 1% expense ratio charges $10 annually for every $1,000 invested. Larger portfolios mean higher absolute costs: $100,000 invested at 1% incurs $1,000 per year in fees, regardless of whether the investments perform well.

While 1% may not sound like much, compare it to a low-cost index fund charging only 0.10%. Over 30 years, the difference becomes dramatic. If both funds return an average of 7% before fees, $10,000 grows to about $54,300 with the 0.10% fund but only around $45,300 with the 1% fund — a difference of $9,000 just from fees. This gap widens further with larger amounts and longer horizons. The higher the fees, the more your compounding returns are reduced.

Fees don't end with expense ratios. Some investment products have sales loads — one-time commissions that can take 3% to 6% off the top when you buy, or when you sell. For a $10,000 investment, that's $300 to $600 gone before your money even has a chance to grow. Ask if the fund charges any entry or exit fees, and favor no-load funds whenever possible.

Hidden and Overlooked Costs

Not every cost shows up on a product sheet. Brokerage commissions, though lower today thanks to zero-commission trading on many platforms, can still add up for frequent traders or those using specialized products. Account maintenance fees — such as annual charges or inactivity fees — may quietly drain accounts, especially smaller ones or those held in specialized accounts like retirement plans.

Taxes loom large as a hidden cost. When investments generate interest, dividends, or realized capital gains, a portion may go to the government. For example, selling a stock that has doubled in value triggers capital gains tax, reducing your net profit. Frequent fund turnover inside actively managed funds can result in higher taxes passed along to investors, even if they haven't personally sold any assets.

Imagine a portfolio producing a pre-tax return of 7%. If annual taxes and hidden fees reduce this by just 1%, the long-term growth drops significantly. Compounded over 20 or 30 years, seemingly minor costs erode a substantial part of the total investment.

Ask for a breakdown of all potential account fees before investing. Review fund documents for trading costs and turnover rates. Use online fee calculators to estimate the total cost year by year. Always check if an account charges for paper statements, wire transfers, or other services.

The True Cost of Overtrading

Frequent buying and selling, often in pursuit of quick gains or to follow the latest trend, comes with a tangible cost. Each trade may incur commissions or spread costs (the difference between buying and selling prices). More importantly, short-term trades often result in short-term taxable gains, which are taxed at a higher rate than long-term holdings.

Research consistently shows that investors who trade often tend to underperform buy-and-hold investors. This underperformance comes from a combination of transaction costs, taxes, and the tendency for frequent traders to mistime the market.

Consider two investors, each starting with $50,000. One trades actively, making 20 trades a year at $10 per trade, plus incurring 1% in taxable short-term gains. The other makes only one or two trades annually and holds investments for the long term, paying little in commissions and enjoying the lower long-term capital gains tax rate. Over a decade, the active trader can lose thousands in extra costs and taxes while also risking lower market returns due to mistimed decisions.

A guiding principle is to trade only when there's a clear, rational reason — such as adjusting for major life changes, rebalancing, or responding to significant shifts in goals or risk tolerance. Before executing a trade, ask yourself: Does this move serve a long-term plan, or is it a reaction to short-term noise?

Cost-Conscious Investing in Practice

To build a cost-efficient portfolio, start by listing all possible fees for each investment option. Compare expense ratios, account fees, and likely tax implications. Use online tools like fee comparison calculators or portfolio analysis apps to see how small differences in cost add up over time. Ask advisors: What is the total cost of owning this investment for five, ten, or thirty years? Are there lower-cost alternatives with similar performance?

Focus on minimizing new trades. Set guidelines such as requiring a written reason for every trade or waiting a week before acting on any new investment idea. Favor diversified, low-cost funds or ETFs, and consider tax-efficient investment accounts. Regularly review statements for new or increasing fees.

Every percentage point saved grows your wealth faster. By making cost-awareness a habit, investors keep more of what they earn and avoid mistakes that quietly drain progress toward their goals.

SPOTTING SCAMS AND AVOIDING BAD ADVICE

Every investor hopes to grow their money safely, but the investment world contains hidden traps. While high fees can eat away at your returns, deliberate scams and bad advice can cause even bigger losses. Understanding the types of fraud and how to protect yourself is just as important as choosing the right stocks or funds.

Recognizing Investment Scams

Investment scams often use the excitement of high profits or new opportunities to draw people in. Some of the most common schemes include Ponzi schemes, pump-and-dump operations, and fake investment opportunities:

- **Ponzi schemes** promise big returns with little risk and generate "profits" by using money from new investors to pay earlier participants. Bernie Madoff's massive fraud is a well-known example, but many smaller versions target ordinary people every year.
- **Pump-and-dump operations** involve hyping up a stock (often through social media or emails) to drive up its price, then the fraudsters sell their shares, making a profit while everyone else is left with worthless stock.
- **Fake investment opportunities** come in many forms — phony real estate deals, fraudulent cryptocurrency schemes, or imaginary startup investments. Scammers create slick websites and convincing materials to make these fake investments seem real.

Spotting Red Flags

Even though scammers routinely update their tactics, there are recognizable warning signs that wise investors learn to spot. Some common red flags include:

- **Promises of guaranteed returns:** No honest investment can promise you a specific profit, especially high or risk-free returns. "No risk, high reward" should always set off alarms.
- **High-pressure sales tactics:** If someone insists you must act immediately or you'll miss out, they may be trying to prevent you from thinking things through or asking questions.

- **Unlicensed or unregistered advisers:** Many scams are operated by advisers or companies with no legal credentials or official registration.
- **Complex, difficult-to-understand strategies:** Scammers often try to confuse victims with jargon or complicated explanations so you feel embarrassed asking questions.
- **Exclusive or time-sensitive opportunities:** If only you are "special enough" for an opportunity, or there's a ticking clock, step back and verify the claims.

Evaluating Financial Advisers and Information

Before working with someone who will handle your investments or advise you what to buy, it's essential to check their background and qualifications. There are clear steps you can take:

Credentials and Registrations

Always ask for proof that advisers are registered with the proper financial authorities. In many countries, advisers must be licensed. In the US, for example, registration with the Securities and Exchange Commission (SEC) or the Financial Industry Regulatory Authority (FINRA) is required for many professionals.

Background Checks

Many countries provide free tools to look up financial advisers. In the US, you can check the SEC's Investment Adviser Public Disclosure website or FINRA's BrokerCheck database. These sites reveal if a person or company has a clean disciplinary record.

Questions to Ask

- What are your credentials and licenses?
- How are you compensated?
- Are you required to put my interests ahead of your own (fiduciary duty)?
- Can you provide references?

Reliable Information Sources

Be wary of viral articles, aggressive salespeople, or self-proclaimed experts without proven backgrounds. Trusted financial news outlets, government resources, and large, reputable financial institutions are safer sources for investment information.

Real-World Scams in Action

A retiree receives a phone call about a "can't-miss" overseas real estate deal, with promises of double-digit annual returns. The salesperson insists she must wire funds within 24 hours. Eager for secure income, she sends money — then never hears from the "firm" again. Or, a social media group hypes a little-known stock. Dozens of individuals buy in, the price surges for days, then collapses. The group moderators, the true orchestrators, disappear after cashing out at the top.

Steps for Due Diligence

Before making any investment, take deliberate steps:

- Research the company or adviser fully.
- Use databases to verify their identity and registration.
- Never invest under pressure; give yourself time to review details.
- Make sure you understand how the investment works and what fees are involved.
- Talk to others who have invested or seek advice from a third, unrelated party.
- Trust your instincts — if anything feels off, seek more information.

Table: Scam Red Flags vs. Legitimate Investments

Aspect	Scam	Legitimate Investment
Guarantees	Promised high, risk-free returns	Never guarantees
Pressure	Urgent, pushy to "act now"	Allows time for decisions
Registration	Unlicensed, can't provide credentials	Fully registered professionals
Clarity	Confusing, vague, or secretive	Explains details openly
Exclusivity	"Only for you," "once-in-a-lifetime"	Publicly available as an option

Trustworthy investments can always withstand your questions. Knowledge, skepticism, and careful research are your best shields against those hoping to trick you out of your hard-earned money.

Now that we understand the common emotional traps, hidden costs, and potential scams that can undermine our investing efforts, we are better equipped to make smart, confident decisions. By recognizing fear, FOMO, and panic before they take over, minimizing fees and unnecessary trades, and staying alert to red flags of fraud, we create a strong foundation for long-term success. With careful planning, patience, and a clear mind, anyone — whether just starting out or looking to grow wealth steadily — can navigate the investment world safely and build a brighter financial future.

SEVEN
GROWING WEALTH OVER THE LONG TERM

Have you ever felt unsure about when to start investing or worried that putting money into the market at the wrong time could cost you dearly? Maybe you've wondered how some people manage to grow their savings steadily while others get stuck watching prices rise and fall, unsure what to do next. Building wealth over time can be confusing, especially if you're new to investing or balancing income from different jobs.

Many people face the challenge of learning how to make consistent, smart financial decisions without becoming overwhelmed by market ups and downs. Beyond simply choosing investments, there's also the question of how to plan for long-term goals like retirement, keep more of your earnings by managing taxes wisely, and track your progress without feeling lost or frustrated. This chapter focuses on practical ways to handle each of these areas, helping you build steady habits and strategies to grow your financial future with confidence.

EMPLOYING FOUNDATIONAL INVESTING STRATEGIES: DOLLAR-COST AVERAGING AND TAX-EFFICIENCY

Many people believe investing is risky because they worry about buying at the "wrong time." Dollar-cost averaging offers a simple solution. Instead of trying to predict when to invest, you decide to invest a fixed amount of money on a regular schedule, such as monthly or every paycheck. This method helps you buy more shares when prices are low and fewer when they are high. Over time, your average cost per share may be lower than if you tried to buy at specific times.

Imagine someone named Ana who decides to invest $100 at the start of each month in a global stock fund. In January, the fund price is $10 per share, so she buys 10 shares. In February, the price drops to $8, so her $100 buys 12.5 shares. In March, the price rises to $12, so she gets 8.33 shares. After three months, Ana has invested $300, and she owns 30.83 shares in total. Her average price per share is about $9.73, even though the share price fluctuated between $8 and $12. By spreading out her investments, Ana doesn't stress about timing the market perfectly.

Dollar-cost averaging works for investors at any income level. Whether you're investing $25 or $1,000 per month, the principle stays the same. This approach helps reduce the impact of sudden market swings and smooths out the ride, holding less risk than investing all your money at once.

Step-by-step Example of Dollar-Cost Averaging

1. Choose an amount you can comfortably invest each month (for example, $100).
2. Select an investment, such as a diversified stock or bond fund.
3. Set up automatic transfers so your money is invested on the same date each month.
4. Over time, record how many shares you buy each month.
5. Add up your total number of shares and the total amount invested. Divide your total investment by the number of shares to see your average cost per share.

By following these steps, you avoid buying everything at high prices and lessen the risk from short-term drops. This can be especially comforting during uncertain times.

Dollar-Cost Averaging: Up and Down Markets

Suppose prices fall for several months. With dollar-cost averaging, you'll end up buying more shares at lower prices. When the market eventually rebounds, the shares you have gathered at bargain prices can boost your returns. If prices rise steadily, dollar-cost averaging means your average purchase price climbs gradually as well, so you never spend all your money at the higher peak.

Mathematically, this method can be shown with a simple calculation. Let's say you invest $100 across four months, with share prices at $10, $8, $12, and $10. You buy 10, 12.5, 8.33, and 10 shares each month. Your total investment is $400, and you end up with about 40.83 shares. Your average price paid: $400 ÷ 40.83 ≈ $9.80. This average is lower than the highest price you would have paid if you invested all at once.

Why It's Ideal for New Investors

For newcomers, dollar-cost averaging lowers the stress of starting your investment journey. You don't need to be an expert or guess the best time to invest. Automatic investing also builds healthy financial habits, encouraging you to stick to your plan and grow your wealth over the long term.

Tax-Efficient Investing Strategies

Building wealth isn't just about investing but about keeping more of what you earn. Taxes can take a surprising bite out of investment gains. Tax-efficient investing helps you minimize that bite and allows your money to grow faster.

Every investor, regardless of country, can benefit from basic tax strategies. Start by using tax-advantaged accounts whenever possible. For example, many countries offer retirement accounts where your investments can grow tax-free or tax-deferred. In these accounts, you might not pay taxes on your investment returns every year; instead, you might pay tax only when you withdraw the money, hopefully in retirement when your tax rate may be lower.

Choosing tax-efficient investment vehicles is another important strategy. Index funds and exchange-traded funds (ETFs) tend to generate fewer taxable events because they buy and sell investments less frequently. Holding investments for the long term can also reduce your taxes, since many countries tax long-term investment gains at a lower rate.

How to Take Action

- Use retirement accounts and tax-free savings vehicles where available
- Favor lower-turnover funds, like ETFs or index funds.
- Hold investments longer to benefit from lower long-term tax rates
- Keep records of investments for easy tax reporting

Common Pitfalls

Many new investors forget about taxes until it's time to sell or withdraw funds. This can lead to unpleasant surprises. By considering taxes from the start, tracking contributions, and understanding your country's tax laws, you can avoid costly mistakes.

No matter your income or investment amount, dollar-cost averaging and tax-efficiency strategies help grow wealth steadily, setting the stage for future financial security and retirement peace of mind.

ALIGNING INVESTMENTS WITH RETIREMENT GOALS

Thinking about retirement might seem far off, but the choices made today have a real impact on life decades in the future. The key to financial safety in retirement is understanding the lifestyle you want and planning investments to make it possible. Start by asking simple but important questions: What age do you want to retire? Do you plan to travel? Will you downsize your home or move to a new location?

Will you have family or medical responsibilities to consider? Mapping out these details provides a clearer target for the amount of money needed.

Estimating living costs in retirement can be straightforward. List your expected monthly expenses, such as housing, food, healthcare, entertainment, transportation, and insurance. Add a buffer for unexpected costs — medical emergencies, home repairs, or changes in family circumstances. Use today's prices, but consider inflation. For example, if current expenses total $3,000 per month, plan for a 2–3% increase yearly to keep pace with rising costs. Multiply annual expenses by the number of years you expect to be retired; this gives a starting place for your savings goal.

After you've settled on a lifestyle estimate, figure out the investment return needed to reach this goal. Consider how much you can save each year and the number of years until you want to stop working. Online retirement calculators let you adjust for varying savings rates, inflation, and expected rates of return, showing how each factor affects your bottom line. For instance, saving $5,000 a year for 30 years with an average return of 6% will build nearly $400,000 before taxes. If cutting expenses or delaying retirement by five years increases your return or savings, it significantly boosts the final amount.

Choosing the right account for your retirement savings is just as important as the amount you save. Traditional individual retirement accounts (IRAs) and workplace 401(k) plans are popular. These accounts often allow pre-tax contributions, which lowers your taxable income now, although you'll pay taxes on withdrawals later. Roth IRAs and Roth 401(k)s let you contribute after-tax dollars, but withdrawals in retirement are tax-free. Freelancers and gig workers may use SEP IRAs or Solo 401(k)s, which offer higher contribution limits and flexibility.

Account Type	Contribution Type	Tax on Growth	Tax on Withdrawals	Who's Eligible
401(k)	Pre-tax/Roth	Tax-deferred	Taxed/Roth-free	Employees, some self-employed
Traditional IRA	Pre-tax	Tax-deferred	Taxed	Anyone with earned income
Roth IRA	After-tax	Grows tax-free	Tax-free	Those under income limits
SEP IRA	Pre-tax	Tax-deferred	Taxed	Self-employed, small business
Solo 401(k)	Pre-tax/Roth	Tax-deferred	Taxed/Roth-free	Self-employed

Choosing between these options depends on your tax situation, work status, and how much flexibility you need. A young professional might start with a Roth IRA for its tax-free growth and easier withdrawals in retirement, while a freelancer with variable income could benefit from a SEP IRA because of its higher contribution limits.

How you divide your investments among stocks, bonds, and cash — known as asset allocation — determines both your level of risk and potential returns. Younger investors can generally afford to invest more heavily in stocks, which carry higher risk but also higher long-term returns. As retirement nears, most people prefer to shift toward bonds and cash for more stability and predictable income. For example, someone in their twenties might use an 80% stock and 20% bond allocation, while a new retiree might hold 40% in stocks, 50% in bonds, and 10% in cash.

It's important to adjust this mix as you approach retirement, gradually reducing risk by shifting from stocks toward bonds and cash. Many investors choose target-date funds, which automatically adjust the allocation based on your expected retirement year.

Small mistakes can undermine years of careful planning. One common pitfall is ignoring inflation, which erodes the value of money over time.

Another is tapping into retirement savings too soon, resulting in penalties and lost growth. Underestimating healthcare costs is also risky. Avoid investing too conservatively early in your career, as this limits growth potential. Overestimating your ability to "catch up" later often leads to disappointment.

When you're finally ready to use your retirement savings, structure your withdrawals to last. Combining Social Security, investment income, and personal savings helps cover expenses. Many retirees use the "4% rule" — withdrawing 4% of their portfolio each year as income — to help make savings last roughly 25 years. Others opt for systematic withdrawals, annuities, or converting part of their investments to cash.

Consistent investment habits, smart account choices, the right mix of assets, and a willingness to adjust along the way put retirement goals within reach. Successful retirement planning means checking your portfolio and progress regularly and making necessary changes if your target or circumstances shift. This careful attention ties retirement security with ongoing performance tracking and ensures you'll stay on course as life changes.

TRACKING AND EVALUATING FINANCIAL PROGRESS

Watching your investments grow over time can be motivating, but successful long-term investors know progress requires more than checking account balances. An effective approach to measuring financial growth starts with selecting the right metrics, then setting up a system for tracking those metrics regularly — without letting emotions drive your decision-making. Productive tracking means monitoring your progress with clear, healthy routines, rather than reacting to every market bump or dip.

Key Performance Indicators for Long-Term Investors

Focusing on a few well-chosen indicators gives a clearer picture of progress. Net worth is a fundamental metric. This is the value of all your assets — like retirement accounts, investment portfolios, and real estate — minus debts. Tracking net worth over time shows whether you're moving closer to your retirement goal, even during periods of market volatility.

Annualized return is another essential indicator. It measures the average yearly gain or loss on your investments, smoothing out short-term ups and downs so you can see long-term trends. Portfolio growth relative to inflation is also important, since growth above inflation reflects real increases in purchasing power.

Asset allocation — the percentage of stocks, bonds, cash, and other asset types — is adjustable and should match your risk tolerance and time frame. Monitoring this balance helps ensure you stay invested in a way that reflects your goals.

Practical Tools and Tracking Methods

You don't need advanced software to monitor financial progress effectively. Many investors use spreadsheets to list accounts, assets, and debts, updating the sheet every quarter or twice yearly. Free online tools from brokerages and personal finance apps can link all accounts in one place and show net worth and performance at a glance.

Regular check-ins work best when you set planned intervals — monthly for checking overall account balances, quarterly for reviewing performance and asset allocation, and annually for a more profound review such as rebalancing. For example, you might review your portfolio performance and contributions on the first Saturday of every quarter and rebalance your investments every January.

A sample review schedule looks like this:

Interval	Actions	Why It Matters
Monthly	Check account balances	Stay aware, avoid surprises
Quarterly	Review returns, asset allocation	Keep on track with goals
Annually	Rebalance, set new goals	Adjust to life changes

Recognizing Warning Signs

Certain signs suggest it's time to review your plan outside of regular intervals. Large, unexpected changes in net worth that aren't tied to market swings, repeated failure to meet savings or contribution targets, or portfolio drift — where your actual investment mix is much different from your target — require a closer look.

In contrast, seeing your account balance drop during a market downturn isn't usually a cause for alarm as long as your investment approach matches your risk preference and time frame. Markets move up and down in the short term; what matters is the long-term trend.

Red Flags vs. Normal Behavior

Red Flags:

- Missing several planned contributions in a row
- Sudden, unexplained drops in net worth
- Asset allocation falling out of alignment significantly (e.g., stocks go from 60% to 80% of your portfolio)
- Strong urge to withdraw or radically change investments based on news headlines

Normal Market Changes:

- Seeing portfolio values fluctuate week-to-week
- Short-term underperformance compared to past years
- Several months of flat or negative growth during overall market corrections

Healthy Monitoring Habits and Avoiding Pitfalls

Healthy investors use scheduled reviews, not impulsive checks. Obsessively checking balances daily — or worse, multiple times daily — can lead to hasty, emotion-driven trades. A study habit is to check no more than once a month for balances and once a quarter for more profound reviews.

It's natural to feel uneasy during market drops, but anxiety can lead to selling at a loss or abandoning a well-planned strategy. Keeping a written investment policy helps; for example, note that your plan is long-term, with a set asset mix, and changes are only made during your scheduled annual review.

Setting Meaningful Benchmarks

Comparing your portfolio to a broad market index, like the S&P 500 for stocks or a balanced index for diversified investors, offers useful context. However, always relate benchmarks to your personal goals — like reaching a set nest egg by retirement age — rather than trying to outpace every market move.

The Role of Rebalancing and Handling Volatility

Rebalancing means adjusting investments to return to your target mix. If stocks rise sharply and become too large a portion of your portfolio, selling some and buying more of other asset classes keeps your risk level steady. Rebalancing once or twice a year is usually enough.

Finally, treat market volatility as normal. Remind yourself that short-term swings don't define long-term outcomes, and sticking to your routine is usually the best way to make progress toward your financial goals.

Now that you understand how proven investment strategies like dollar-cost averaging and tax-efficient planning work, you are better equipped to build steady, long-term wealth without the stress of market timing or unexpected tax surprises. By aligning your investments with clear retirement goals and consistently tracking your progress using simple tools, you can make informed decisions that keep you on course even when markets fluctuate. Remember, investing is a journey that rewards patience, regular habits, and smart adjustments as your life and goals evolve. With these methods in place, you can confidently take control of your financial future and watch your money grow over time.

EIGHT
YOUR INVESTOR MINDSET

Have you ever felt overwhelmed by the idea of investing, unsure where to begin or how to stay steady when markets swing wildly? Maybe you've wondered why some people seem to grow their wealth patiently over time, while others chase quick wins that come and go. It's easy to get caught up in daily price changes and headlines, losing sight of what truly matters for building lasting financial security.

The way you think about investing shapes not only your decisions but also your ability to stick with a plan through uncertain times. Developing the right mindset can transform investing from a stressful guessing game into a purposeful path toward your goals. This chapter invites you to explore how embracing long-term thinking, managing emotions, and connecting your investments to the life you want can set the foundation for success.

ADOPTING A LONG-TERM INVESTMENT PERSPECTIVE

Imagine you're choosing between planting a vegetable seed or buying salad from the store every day. Going with the seed takes patience — watering it, waiting, and watching it grow. Buying salad gives instant results but nothing for tomorrow. This is the difference between short-term and long-term investing. Day traders are like salad buyers, looking for quick gains by frequently buying and selling stocks. They focus on rapid swings, news headlines, and daily price changes, hoping to snatch small profits before moving on. Long-term investors, on the other hand, are gardeners. They buy shares in strong companies and hold those investments through sunny and stormy days, trusting that their value will rise over years, not minutes.

Long-term thinking isn't just about waiting; it's a mindset shift. Setting realistic timeframes is the foundation. If you're saving for a house in five years or building retirement wealth over decades, you tailor your investment plan to your unique timeline. It helps to write down specific goals: "I want to buy a home in 7 years," or "I'm building a retirement fund for age 65." These clear targets anchor you during volatile markets and help turn dreams into actionable plans.

One of the most powerful tools for long-term investors is compound interest. Think of it like rolling a snowball down a hill — it gets bigger faster the farther it travels. If you invest $5,000 at a 7% annual return and leave it alone, it grows not just from your original money, but from the earnings it makes each year. Over 20 years, that $5,000 can more than triple, all without you lifting a finger. The earlier you start, the bigger the snowball.

Price and value are often mistaken for the same thing, but there's an important difference. Price is what you pay for a share at any moment — like a sticker on a shirt at the mall. The shirt's value is its quality and longevity. Just because a stock's price drops or rises doesn't always mean its underlying value changed. Savvy investors look for quality companies that are underpriced relative to their potential, not just bargains on sale.

Emotions can sabotage even the best investment plans. When markets tumble, fear whispers, "Sell before it gets worse." When stocks surge, greed urges you to chase the hottest trend. Both can lead to costly decisions. Notice when your heartbeat rises as you check your investment app or when "doom-and-gloom" headlines get your attention. Taking a deep breath and remembering your long-term goals can serve as your initial defense.

Here are some actionable ways to build investment patience and discipline:

- Spend 15 minutes each week reviewing your goals instead of your portfolio's daily ups and downs.
- Create a simple habit: before making any investment move, wait 24 hours and write down your reasons for acting.
- Use automatic investing features to put away a fixed amount each month without thinking about market timing.

A helpful framework for decision-making is the checklist approach:

Simple Decision-Making Framework

Step	Action
1	Identify your goal and timeline
2	Research the investment's fundamentals (earnings, stability, history)
3	Ask if the price is attractive compared to its long-term value
4	Assess if the investment fits your broader portfolio
5	Pause, reflect, and then act rather than react

Consider these everyday scenarios:

A young professional opens a retirement account and consistently contributes a portion of every paycheck. Instead of jumping in and out of stocks based on market news, she trusts in the slow, steady climb of long-term growth. Years later, she finds her account much larger than friends who tried to time the market.

A freelancer enjoys irregular income. Instead of waiting for a big lump sum, he sets up an automatic transfer of whatever he can spare each month into a diversified fund. This keeps his investing habit alive, regardless of how busy or slow his business gets.

Someone with a side hustle decides that for every $100 earned, $20 goes into an index fund. Over five years, the discipline pays off, turning those small, regular investments into a solid nest egg.

Many worry that long-term investing means missing out on quicker money. However, research shows fewer trades often lead to lower taxes, decreased fees, and less emotional burnout. Market swings happen, but history demonstrates that patient investors who ride out volatility usually come out ahead.

Markets will always have ups and downs. Uncertainty is part of the journey, not a sign to panic. If you treat investing like planting a tree — nurturing it and waiting for its shade — rather than chasing every passing trend, you prepare yourself for healthier financial growth. wealthier future. Take small, thoughtful steps and trust in the process. The rewards build up, just like a seed becoming a tree.

NAVIGATING VOLATILITY & EMBRACING LIFELONG LEARNING

Markets move up and down for many reasons. Some days bring small, routine changes, while at other times larger swings can happen suddenly. This movement is called volatility. Volatility measures how much and how quickly prices change, and it comes in different forms. Normal volatility includes everyday ups and downs as investors react to news, company reports, or shifts in interest rates. Abnormal volatility, on the other hand, is less common and occurs during major events such as global crises or financial crashes, when prices move sharply in a short period.

Throughout history, the stock market has always moved in cycles. The financial crisis of 2008, the dot-com bubble burst in the early 2000s, and the COVID-19 market drop in 2020 all remind us that sharp declines can and do happen. Each time, investors who stayed patient eventually saw the markets recover. Successful long-term investors understand that downturns are part of the process. After most drops, markets have not only rebounded but often reached new highs, rewarding those who stayed invested. Recognizing the difference between short-term panic and lasting change is essential. A bad headline might send prices down briefly, but unless there's a deeper problem, it's usually just normal market movement.

When investments lose value, emotions can run high. Fear, anxiety, and frustration are common during market declines. These feelings can lead investors to sell at a loss or abandon their strategy altogether. Recognizing emotional triggers is the first step toward regaining control. Common triggers include seeing a negative account balance, hearing alarming news, or comparing losses with others. To manage emotions, pause and take a breath. Remind yourself why you invested and remember that downturns are temporary. Many investors use written plans to stay grounded, reviewing their long-term goals whenever fear starts to rise.

Several specific techniques can help maintain composure. Limiting how often you check your investment accounts helps avoid unnecessary stress. Setting up automatic contributions keeps your investment plan on track, even when headlines are dramatic. Another tool is "reframing": instead of seeing a drop as a loss, view it as a temporary dip and a possible buying opportunity. When in doubt, reach out to a mentor or a trusted advisor for perspective. Sticking to your plan, especially when it's tested by volatility, is one of the most powerful habits of successful investors. Research shows that most people who panic-sell regret it later, missing out on rebounds.

A simple framework for responding to volatility can make decisions easier during stressful times. Start with clear rules: decide in advance under what conditions you would make changes to your portfolio. For example, some changes are only warranted if your goals change, or if one part of your portfolio grows much larger than planned. Use checklists to avoid emotional decisions. Before acting, ask a few guiding questions: Did your financial needs change? Did something fundamental in the market or your investments shift for the long term?

Is this a rare, historic event or a normal part of the investment cycle? If the answer is no, holding steady is usually the smarter move.

Acting out of fear often leads to trouble, while disciplined investors benefit from patience. It's important to balance awareness with discipline. Occasionally, a major life change or a clear sign of trouble in a company or economy means you should adjust your plan. But most of the time, sticking with your original strategy works best. Reviewing your investments regularly — once or twice a year — is often enough. When in doubt, refer back to your personal investment goals, not the market's mood.

To make sense of what's happening without getting overwhelmed, rely on a few trusted information sources. Financial news from well-known sites, official market summaries, and reports from respected advisors can keep you informed. Ignore day-to-day noise from social media or opinion-based commentary that stirs fear or hype. Set time limits for reading market news and focus on data over drama. Write down important signals, such as changes to interest rates or official company updates. Limit checking portfolio values to a regular schedule — weekly or monthly instead of daily — to keep perspective.

Real-world examples offer proof that these strategies work. During the 2020 pandemic crash, investors who stayed invested through the drop saw their portfolios recover within months. Those who pulled out missed the upswing. Warren Buffett is known for his calm approach, famously saying to "be fearful when others are greedy and greedy when others are fearful." Many professionals avoid emotional pitfalls by sticking to decision-making frameworks.

Managing market volatility is a lifelong skill. Every cycle brings new lessons. Ongoing learning and reflection help you stay prepared, turning each market swing into a chance for growth and improvement as an investor.

USING INVESTMENT TO CREATE FREEDOM AND FULFILLMENT

Choosing to invest is about more than growing money. It's a way to build the kind of life you really want. When you step into investing, you adopt habits that reach far past your portfolio. Discipline, patience, and the drive to keep learning can shape your everyday choices, helping you become more intentional about life itself.

You may have already started asking yourself what truly matters to you. Begin simply. Set aside ten minutes with a notebook. List the moments in your life when you felt happiest, proudest, and most fulfilled. What do these memories have in common? Maybe you see adventure, family time, autonomy, or creativity popping up again and again. These patterns point directly to your core values.

Once you've prioritized your values, consider your most ambitious aspirations. Do you crave freedom to live anywhere? Time for creative projects? The security to weather unexpected changes? Turn these aspirations into clear statements. "I want to live in a new city every year." "I want to switch careers without worrying about my bills." "I want to retire while I still have energy to travel." When you can see the life you want in words, it becomes easier to map out the steps to getting there.

Translating values and aspirations into financial goals is next. If you desire location independence, you might set a goal of building a portfolio that generates steady passive income. Are you dreaming of an early retirement? Determine the amount you'll need to support your lifestyle, then break that number down into yearly savings and investment targets. An engineer who values flexibility could prioritize a sturdy emergency fund alongside investments in broad market index funds — tools that support smooth transitions if they want to take a career break or freelance.

Examples make the process real. Consider Maya, who loves travel and personal growth. She invests in dividend-paying stocks and real estate funds that provide regular income. She spends a few months each year living abroad, confident her investment income can support her adventures. Alex, seeking early retirement, follows a disciplined savings plan. He invests aggressively in tax-advantaged retirement accounts and automates regular contributions to keep on track. Instead of guessing, he calculates exactly how much he'll need each month and adjusts his portfolio every year based on his progress and changes in his goals.

Aligning your investments with your life vision isn't just for the wealthy or financial experts. Ordinary people constantly do this, in ways that fit their means and dreams. Parents who want to work less while their children are young might invest in rental properties. A freelance designer could build a small cash cushion before leaping into self-employment, investing the rest in low-cost funds to grow slowly over time. The goal is always the same: give your investments a job that serves your unique goals.

You can follow a clear process to keep your investing in sync with your life direction:

1. Identify your core values and aspirations.
2. Define specific lifestyle goals that reflect these values.
3. Calculate the financial requirements for each goal.
4. Choose investment strategies that best match your goals.
5. Set up automatic contributions or investment plans to stay consistent.
6. Review your progress and update your plan as needed.

Here's what this looks like in practice. Start with a worksheet or spreadsheet where you list each goal, the estimated cost, and the timeline. For example:

Goal	Estimated Cost	Timeline	Investment Strategy
Year-long world travel	$30,000	2 years	Short-term bond funds
Mini-retirement in 5 years	$120,000	5 years	Balanced mutual funds, CDs
Flexible remote work	$15,000	1 year	High-yield savings, ETFs

Every six to twelve months, revisit your sheet. Are your priorities changing? Did you reach one goal and now want to set your sights higher? Maybe your income increased, letting you invest more, or a new interest popped up that shifts your plans. Adjust your targets, rebalance your portfolio, and celebrate milestones along the way.

Building wealth is most rewarding when your money is doing more than multiplying on a statement. It's a tool for freedom, personal growth, and peace of mind. When you make investing a conscious part of your life design, you move closer to living each day on your own terms.

Start now. Reflect on what freedom and fulfillment truly mean to you. Make your list of core values and dreams, translate them into specific financial actions, and take that first step. Each dollar invested with a purpose is a step toward the life you envision.

Now that you understand the mindset needed for long-term investing, you can approach your financial journey with patience and confidence, knowing that staying focused on your goals will help you navigate market ups and downs without panic. By adopting habits like setting clear objectives, avoiding emotional reactions, and using automatic contributions, you create a steady path toward building wealth that supports the life you want. Remember, investing is more than just growing money — it's about creating freedom, resilience, and fulfillment in your everyday life. As you move forward, keep learning, stay disciplined, and trust in the process, knowing that every thoughtful step brings you closer to a secure and rewarding financial future.

YOUR FEEDBACK, THEIR FIRST STEP

Every time we share what we've learned, we light the path for someone else who may feel lost.

Have you ever wished you had clear guidance when you first started learning about money, investing, or building a financial future?

Imagine a young professional who wants to invest but feels overwhelmed by jargon, or a gig worker who wants to save for stability but isn't sure where to begin. For them, your perspective could be the spark of encouragement they need.

If *Investing 101* helped you feel more confident about investing — whether by simplifying the basics, showing you practical strategies, or helping you see that even small steps can lead to long-term growth — I'd be deeply grateful if you left an honest review.

Your feedback doesn't just help me improve; it helps future readers decide whether this book could give them the clarity and courage they need to begin their own journey toward financial independence.

Thank you so much for reading, reflecting, and — if you choose — sharing your thoughts. Your words have the power to guide others toward building the security and freedom they deserve.

CONCLUSION

You've reached the final page of this book, and it's a moment worth celebrating. Maybe you picked up these chapters feeling uncertain, maybe even intimidated — wondering if investing was only for wealthy experts or intimidating professionals in expensive suits. If you've ever thought that building wealth was something out of your reach, this journey should have painted a different picture: investing isn't about where you start — it's about moving forward, one step at a time, with confidence.

Over these pages, we've broken down the world of investing into its most essential pieces. You've learned that financial success isn't about luck, magical timing, or having a giant paycheck. It's built on consistency — showing up for your future self every day, even when it feels like your contributions are small. Simplicity is another foundational brick; you don't need to memorize complex stock charts or follow every twist and turn of the market. The best investors often focus on clear, simple decisions that work for them over time. And perhaps more important than anything else, you've discovered the value of trusting yourself. You can make good choices with your money, you can keep learning, and you can build a solid foundation — no matter where you're starting from today.

Think back to where you were at the beginning of this book. Maybe you saw investing as a winding, misty road filled with jargon and big risks. Now, you know that there's a path forward tailored to real, everyday people: students managing their first paychecks, gig workers collecting payments from multiple side hustles, young professionals balancing career steps with life goals, and anyone else who wants to put their money to work instead of watching it lose value in a checking account. If that sounds like you, know that you're exactly who this book was written for — and that you already have what it takes.

The tools and strategies you've picked up are designed to grow with you, no matter how complicated life becomes. Maybe you'll be working full-time, switching careers, freelancing, or juggling family obligations — all of these paths can support good investing habits. When you stay consistent, setting aside a small part of each paycheck, you send a powerful message to your future self: "I'm making my financial well-being a priority." This isn't about perfection — there will always be curveballs, months tighter than expected, markets that go up and down without warning — but every effort counts, and those little actions add up faster than you'd think.

If you remember just one thing from this book, let it be this: You do not need to have it all figured out before you start. In fact, no one does — not even the seasoned pros. What separates successful investors from everyone else isn't perfect timing or secret knowledge. It's a willingness to learn, to begin, and to course-correct along the way. Every investor, regardless of background or bank balance, has faced fears and doubts. But those feelings don't mean you shouldn't move forward. They're a sign that you care about your future, and that's a powerful motivator.

Don't wait for a perfect moment — because perfect moments rarely show up on schedule. Start with what you have, right now. Even small amounts, invested regularly, have the potential to grow impressively thanks to the power of compounding. Don't underestimate the impact of those first few dollars — or the momentum created by taking action. With every move you make, you gain new insight, confidence, and clarity. Over time, you'll see this process pay off, both financially and in your own sense of empowerment.

Investing isn't just about numbers on a screen or reaching some distant retirement goal. It's about freedom — the freedom to choose work because you want to, not because you have to; the opportunity to support causes you believe in; the ability to weather unexpected changes with stability and peace of mind. Each thoughtful decision you make today lays a stepping stone toward those possibilities.

Of course, your learning doesn't end here. If you're excited to keep going deeper, there are endless resources to help you sharpen your skills — books, podcasts, online courses, investment communities, and financial advisors who specialize in beginners. Seeking out trustworthy information is always a wise move, especially as the world of finance continues to evolve. Remember, staying curious and open-minded is what will keep you growing as an investor. Surround yourself with ideas and people who encourage your progress, not intimidate it.

One practical next step is to set a regular time in your calendar — once a month, or once a quarter — to review your investments and reflect on your progress. Track what's working for you, spot new opportunities, and celebrate your wins, no matter how small. If a certain strategy or tool isn't fitting your life anymore, give yourself permission to adjust. Investing should adapt to you — not the other way around.

For anyone still feeling nervous, trust that the hard part — getting started — is already behind you. You've chosen to educate yourself, to confront your fears, and to take responsibility for your financial destiny. That alone puts you ahead of the curve. While challenges may arise, the clarity and confidence you've gained will serve as steady companions on your journey.

Let's also acknowledge the courage it takes to challenge old ideas about money — perhaps ones you grew up with, or absorbed from pop culture and peers. Maybe you were led to believe that investing is risky, confusing, or only worthwhile if you already have plenty of cash lying around. By finishing this book, you've proven to yourself that you're ready to replace outdated beliefs with facts, strategies, and a genuine belief in your own abilities.

As you close these pages, hold tight to the main themes you've learned: the consistency of small, ongoing action; the beauty of simplicity — choosing investments and routines you understand and can stick with; and above all, self-trust. These qualities will carry you further than any trend or hot tip ever could. Your path will be unique, shaped by your values, responsibilities, and goals. There's no single formula, but there are timeless principles that work for everyone willing to apply them.

The best time to invest in your future is always now. Let this book be your launchpad, your primer, and your reminder that you are more than capable of turning your curiosity into concrete results. Whether you're a recent graduate, a freelancer, a side hustler, or someone simply looking for a better way, you have everything you need to get started — not someday, not after the next raise, but today.

Where you go from here is entirely up to you. Keep asking questions, keep seeking knowledge, and — most importantly — keep taking action. Let your first steps be bold, imperfect, and entirely your own. Investing is a lifelong journey, and you've taken the most important leap: you've begun.

www.ingramcontent.com/pod-product-compliance
Lightning Source LLC
Chambersburg PA
CBHW050531240926
51846CB00003B/773
9781970839036